Egbert C. Smyth

The Andover Heresy

In the Matter of the Complaint against Egbert C. Smyth and others,

professors of the Theological Institution in Phillips academy, Andover

Egbert C. Smyth

The Andover Heresy

In the Matter of the Complaint against Egbert C. Smyth and others, professors of the Theological Institution in Phillips academy, Andover

ISBN/EAN: 9783337191344

Printed in Europe, USA, Canada, Australia, Japan

Cover: Foto ©Lupo / pixelio.de

More available books at **www.hansebooks.com**

The Andover Heresy.

IN THE MATTER OF THE COMPLAINT AGAINST EGBERT C. SMYTH AND OTHERS, PROFESSORS OF THE THEOLOGICAL INSTITUTION IN PHILLIPS ACADEMY, ANDOVER.

PROFESSOR SMYTH'S ARGUMENT,

TOGETHER WITH

THE STATEMENTS OF PROFESSORS TUCKER, HARRIS, HINCKS, AND CHURCHILL.

BOSTON:
CUPPLES, UPHAM & COMPANY,
The Old Corner Bookstore,
283 Washington Street.
1887.

Franklin Press:
RAND AVERY COMPANY,
BOSTON.

IN THE MATTER OF THE COMPLAINT AGAINST EGBERT C. SMYTH AND OTHERS,

Professors of the Theological Institution in Phillips Academy in Andover.

May it please your Reverend and Honorable Body:

By the Statutes of the Associate Foundation it is made your duty "to take care that the duties of every Professor on this Foundation be intelligibly and faithfully discharged, and to admonish or remove him, either for misbehavior, heterodoxy, incapacity, or neglect of the duties of his office." By the Statutes of the Brown Professorship, which I have the honor to hold, this Foundation is made "subject to visitation" in the same manner with the Associate Foundation. In the libel filed by the complainants and which defines the present issue I am not charged with misbehavior, incapacity, or neglect of official duty. The sole issue is one of "heterodoxy."

I desire to call your attention to the fact that I am not charged with "neglect of the duties of my [his] office." It is certainly possible that a Professor, enamored of some new opinion neither out of "harmony with" nor "antagonistic to" the Creed of the Seminary, might spend so much time in maintaining and inculcating it as to neglect his duty in respect to other truths. If this were the accusation in the present case I am confident that I should have no difficulty in meeting it. But wide as is the range of the present libel it nowhere ventures upon such an aspersion. I stand before you, even in these calumnious days, absolutely without reproach from any quarter in this particular.

I am charged before you with "heterodoxy"—nothing more, nothing less, nothing other. If I am guilty of "heterodoxy" you can remove or admonish me as the issue of this trial, according to your judgment and discretion. If I am not guilty I am entitled to a clear acquittal.

It has been said that this is not a trial for heresy, but for a breach of trust. A suit for a breach of trust would lie more properly against the Trustees or Treasurer of the Seminary. Not a cent of the Seminary Funds comes into my hands save as I receive it from said Treasurer, who acts by order of the Trustees. If there has been a breach of trust in the management of the funds the custodians and disbursers of those funds are guilty of this offence, and there are available and natural methods of prosecution. The arraignment of five professors, and the interruption of their work in the midst of a term of study, is not one of these natural methods. This is a trial for heresy, or it is nothing. The violation of solemn promises which is charged is simply an issue of interpretation of a creed. The only charge in essence and in form is the accusation of "heterodoxy."

It may indeed be suggested in qualification of what I have said, that "heterodoxy" in the present instance is to be determined by an unusual, particular and remote standard, and that this criterion is not the test which would now be imposed, so that I might be orthodox according to the rule which would be applied to-day, and yet heterodox according to the rule prescribed in the Seminary Creed. I do not admit that such a distinction is applicable in the present case. I am advised by eminent legal authority that the word "heterodoxy" in the Statutes cannot be thus limited and defined. But irrespective of this objection I must say that I think better of our Creed, better of the Founders of the Seminary, than such a contention would admit. The Creed bears traces, doubtless, of controversies which no longer interest the public, and unadjusted and even irreconcilable conceptions linger in some of its phrases. But to whatever criticisms it is fairly exposed, I "hold, maintain, and inculcate," Mr. President, that it does not bind the Seminary to an antiquated phase of belief, or to the "warts and wens" which a living theology knows how to get rid of, but on the contrary, that it logically leads to those adjustments of orthodox thought and belief which are now necessary, and in general leaves an open path for such as the future may require. Such a statement doubtless will strike with surprise some who are the friends of doctrinal progress. There is abroad an opinion which is founded, I am persuaded, upon *a priori* reasoning, and not upon scientific examination. It is like certain theories of inspiration which are derived from what men think the Bible ought to be and not from what it is. It reasons thus: The human mind has made doctrinal progress since the century opened. A creed written eighty years ago must be antiquated. That depends. An *a priori* "must be," science has taught us, is not always an "is so." It depends on who says it, still more on what has been said. I am not a eulogizer of the Andover Creed. Clothed in phraseology which it requires much special learning accurately to interpret, composed as a compromise, designed to admit under it a great variety of philosophical theories and beliefs, expressive at certain points by its silences even more than by its utterances, balancing traditional statements by novelties of doctrine, inserting some words to bar against regression and others which make progress necessary, confessing the authority of Scripture but not failing to emphasize the constant revelation in creation, providence and redemption, it cannot be rightly understood without a more careful study than its critics have usually given to it, and whatever else it may be I am persuaded that it is not the symbol of an antiquated phase of orthodoxy, nor the chain and ball of an imprisoned theology. I appear before you of necessity to make personal answer to charges most of which are utterly false, charges some of which, if true, would justly expose me to the accusation of heresy under the standards of a catholic orthodoxy, but I have a larger contention and a deeper interest. I desire to secure by your decision for those who may come after me the rights of a reverent scholarship in the study of God's word; the liberties of thought and life which are necessary to fruitful biblical study; the opportunity for that spontaneity and freedom in the discovery and acquisition of sacred truth, without which the articles of any creed however excellent can never become the reality of present, personal convictions and the living springs of knowledge, but must always remain the dry and barren deposit of a dead past. I believe the result at which I aim expresses the only correct interpretation of the duties and rights of a Professor in Andover Seminary, as these obligations and liberties are defined and guaranteed in the Creed and Statutes of the Founders.

Before, however, I venture out upon this larger field of thought, I desire to meet the complainants upon the narrowest line which they may select. I shall attempt to show that, even when every indication from the Founders is disregarded which points to that nobler conception of the function of the Creed at which I have just hinted, the present complaint is still futile and void.

In order to convict me under the present libel the complainants must prove that I hold beliefs which are inconsistent with a valid acceptance of the Creed, or that I have violated my solemn promise "that I will maintain and inculcate the Christian faith as expressed in the Creed . . . so far as may appertain to my office, according to the best light God shall give me, and in opposition to" various heresies and errors specified and unspecified, ancient and modern.

The first requirement pertains to belief, the second to official conduct in matters of faith.

To establish my guilt under the first requirement the complainants must prove at least two things: that I hold an alleged belief, and that this belief is contrary to the Creed. As I have intimated it will be contended in my behalf that there is still a further condition of the validity of the accusation, viz., that this particular belief be shown to be heterodox by a yet higher and more continuous and potent standard of orthodoxy. Without waiving this point I shall not press it in what I here present. I am content to insist at the present stage of the argument upon the two conditions first named, the necessity of proving that I hold what is charged, and that such a belief contravenes the Creed.

To prove my guilt under the second requirement, — that of official conduct, — still more must be established than under the first. My official promise must be considered in all its parts, and as a whole. No one can rob me of the conviction that whatever have been my deficiencies I have endeavored to maintain and inculcate so far as pertains to my office "the fundamental and distinguishing doctrines of the gospel" as expressed in the Creed, "according to the best light God" has given me, and in opposition to the various errors by which history shows that these truths have been confronted. I have preferred, however, to try and show what neglected element of truth heresy may be thriving upon, and how it may be healed by a larger truth, rather than merely to antagonize it. I submit to your careful consideration this test of the validity of any proof, advanced by the complainants, of my "heterodoxy" as a teacher. It is a three-fold cord. Each strand is necessary. It is weak as a broken thread if either fails. It must be shown that I have "maintained and inculcated," that is, taught purposely and urgently, what is charged; that I have done this in my work as a Professor in the Seminary; and that this deed is a violation of my promise to teach the Christian faith as expressed in the Creed "according to the best light God shall give me." I ask you in simple justice rigidly to apply this test to what on this point the complainants may offer as proof.

You will pardon me also if I request you to bear in mind that I am not on trial before you as an editor of the *Andover Review*, or as a joint author of a volume called *Progressive Orthodoxy* published by Messrs. Houghton, Mifflin & Co., 4 Park Street, Boston. I would not draw any fine or artificial distinction between my utterances in the *Review* and in the Lecture Room. No honest man, certainly no trustworthy religious teacher, can hold a double and mutually contradictory set of opinions, one for his pupils, another for his own privacy or for some other use. If I have taught in the *Review* what is contrary to the Creed, I shall not plead that I have been more reserved or utterly silent in my lectures. I have, however, a point to make which may assume importance. It is this. In the field of literature I am amenable to your jurisdiction only so far as it can be proved that what I publish is contrary to the Creed, or actually violates, or necessarily and evidently tends to violate, my obligations as Brown Professor of Ecclesiastical History in the Theological Institution in Phillips Academy in Andover. In a volume or review, for instance, I am perfectly at liberty to dwell *ad libitum* on a single topic. I might co-operate in a temperance journal, or one devoted to Civil Service Reform, and write on one or the other of these subjects every month, provided I neglected none of the duties of my office. Much more on some living theological or religious question, under the same condition. But it would be contrary to the duties of my office to give such prominence to these questions in my lecture room. So far as the *Review* or *Progressive Orthodoxy* is now before you, the issue is not what prominence is given to a subject, but whether any thing is taught which shows a belief or beliefs contrary to the Creed, or a violation of my promise as to conduct in my office.

Indulge me in one other preliminary remark. I regret that the number and variety of the charges in the libel make it impossible for me to be brief. I am charged with heterodoxy upon nearly all the distinguishing doctrines of our Holy Religion. The indictment seems to be constructed on the plan of somebody's note-books of a course of lectures in Systematic Theology, embracing the leading topics from the Being of God to the final resurrection and the contrasted eternal states. One of the signers, in the original complaint, wrote "Trustee" under his name. He is a Trustee of the Seminary, of many years' standing. Being a clergyman he has been very often appointed by his associates to attend my theological examinations. I have almost invariably, from year to year, examined on the Church doctrine of the Trinity. He knows, or is inexcusable if he does not know, what I have taught. He knows, or ought to know, that I have taught from year to year the doctrine of the Trinity, the Church doctrine; and that I "hold, maintain and inculcate" it, as I have done all along. I am thankful that it does not devolve upon me to occupy your time in trying to explain why he has deemed it necessary to sign his name, in the professed interest of honesty of subscription, to a charge that I teach a modal Trinity, a charge which he knows full well, or is inexcusable if he does not know, is baseless and false, but unless he and his associates withdraw this charge and others equally preposterous, I must take time to refute them. Fortunately for the demands upon your time the strength of the list is in inverse ratio to its length.

Believing that you will appreciate the necessity laid upon me of reviewing in detail and with thoroughness these numerous accusations, and reminding you again of the two-fold, or three-fold necessities of evidence adequate to establish any one of these charges, I now proceed to their consideration.

The *first particular charge* is, that I "hold, maintain and inculcate that the Bible is not 'the only perfect rule of faith and practice,' but is fallible and untrustworthy even in some of its religious teachings."

What has there been in the evidence submitted on this point by the complainants which proves either that I hold what is charged, or that there is any thing in the article or citations adduced which affords any presumption that I thus teach, or that any thing which I teach or for which I am responsible is contrary to the Creed? I have not been able to detect a scintilla of evidence for either of these positions, each and all of which must be established or the charge falls.

Take first the article in the *Review* entitled "The Bible a Theme for the Pulpit." How or where does this show that, so far as appertains to my office, I fail in upholding the supreme authority of sacred Scripture? In what lies the proof that in the chapel pulpit, or in my lecture room, or in any public utterance whatsoever, I oppose the declaration of the Creed "that the word of God contained in the Scriptures of the Old and New Testaments is the only perfect rule of faith and practice"? Not only is no connection of this sort traced by the complainants, they have done nothing to lay the foundation for a presumption or suggestion in favor of such a connection. For there is no expression anywhere in the article of the thing charged. It contains not a syllable adverse to the requirement of the Creed. On the contrary, the article was written in the interest of the doctrine affirmed in the Creed. Its occasion was the discovery that some ministers, recognizing that many of their hearers hold to the old theory that the Bible in every part is equally authoritative and in every statement is infallible truth, and knowing also that such a proposition cannot be maintained, out of prudential motives have withdrawn from the teachings of the pulpit any instruction as to what the Bible is as the only perfect rule, and how it has become such a rule. The writer endeavored to enter into the thoughts and feelings of such ministers, to appreciate the reasons which influence them, to state those reasons, in order to point out to them that there is a better way, and one which it is the duty of the ministry of intelligent churches to follow. What now is the use made of this article by the complainants? First, five sentences are detached from that portion in which the embarrassments of the preacher are depicted. Then, a skip is made to the close of the article and a sentence picked up and so connected that its object is precisely reversed. It was written as a suggestion, at the close of a brief article, how, by pursuing a particular method of pulpit discussion, men disturbed by the results of modern critical study may be helped to a firm and immovable conviction of the trustworthiness and perfection of sacred Scripture as a rule of faith and practice. It is quoted as though it were designed to favor a treatment of the Bible "prejudicial to its sacredness and authority."

One is reminded that there is still need of the irony with which a bishop of the English Church two centuries ago discoursed upon "The Difficulties and Discouragements which attend the Study of the Scriptures in the way of Private Judgment; Represented in a letter to a young clergyman." He will subject himself to much toil in study, will be likely by the results of his labor to disturb the peace of the church and bring upon himself the reproach of being a *heretic*, "a term which there is a strange magic in. . . . It is supposed to include in it every thing that is bad; it makes every thing appear odious and deformed; it dissolves all friendships, extinguishes all former kind sentiments however just and well deserved. And from the time a man is deemed a heretic, it is charity to act against all the rules of charity; and the more they violate the laws of God in dealing with him, it is, in their opinion, doing God the greater service. . . . A search after truth will be called a love of novelty. The doubting of a single text will be scepticism; the denial of an argument the renouncing of the faith. . . . In a word orthodoxy atones for all vices and heresy extinguishes all virtues. . . . Turn yourself to the study of the heathen historians, poets, orators and philosophers. Spend ten or twelve years upon Horace or Terence. To illustrate a *billet-doux*, or a drunken catch; to explain an obscene jest; to make a happy emendation on a passage that a modest man would blush at, will do you more credit and be of greater service to you, than the most useful employment of your time upon the Scriptures; unless you can resolve to conceal your sentiments, and speak always with the vulgar. . . . You have two ways before you. *One* will enable you to be useful in the world, without great trouble to yourself. . . . The *other* . . . will draw on you an insupportable load of infamy, as a disturber of the church and an enemy to the orthodox faith, and in all probability end in the extreme poverty and ruin of yourself and family. Which God forbid should ever be the case of one who has no other views but to dedicate his life to God's service."

Who has forgotten the abuse which was rained upon Professor Stuart for his biblical studies? Writing (Oct. 7, 1813) to Dr. Spring, the son of a principal author of the Seminary

Creed, he says — referring to the "exegesis of Canticles:" "For my humble self, if I doubt whether the forty-nine senses can all be applied to this book . . . and must be a heretic on this account, I say with Vitringa, *Ego sum in hac hæresi*. . . .

"I certainly," he continues, "do not think it worth the trouble of writing this to save myself from the imputation of heresy, among those who make all divinity heretical that is not *triangular*. . . . 'What, said Father Paoli to his brother Jesuit, who was less dexterous in combating for the mother church than himself. What did Scarpi say at the meeting of the order? — He said he doubted whether the infallibility of the Church could be predicated of the Pope alone, or whether it resided in an ecumenical council. — Most abominable! and what did you tell him? — I told him that the Pope was the successor of St. Peter. — Well, and what said he? — He said that he did not read in the New Testament of Peter's having appointed any successor, and challenged me to produce the passage. — Challenged you to produce the passage! — Yes; and I was not able to recollect it. — Able to recollect it! why did you not tell him that the Fathers believed as we do? — I did. — And what said he? — Why, that the Fathers were not the Pope, and so were not infallible. — Why didn't you tell him that he would endanger the faith of the whole Church by such *innovations?* — I did try to argue with him about them. — *Argue* with him! you stupid blockhead (*fatuus Diaboli*) — *argue with him!* Why did you not call him HERETIC . . . ? These heretics are to be confounded by blows, not by arguments (*fustibus non argumentis confutandos*).'

"Thus," adds Professor Stuart, "believes brother Romeyn, as truly as Father Paoli, and for as good a reason. If you think strange of this, you have only to recollect that two pennyweights of brains are a sufficient apparatus for the purpose of guiding a march through the whole round of hard names and abusive insinuations, while it needs several pounds to manage an argument." . . .

May it please your Reverend and Honorable Body I have searched diligently through the printed specifications under

this charge about the Scriptures, and have listened carefully
to catch any, even the faintest, suggestion of some utterance
for which I am responsible, which militates in the least
against the divine authority of the Scripture, but I have not
discovered it. Where is it found? Is an attempt to show
how a divine revelation has come to us, an attack upon revelation? The most cursory reading of either of the articles
named or cited, shows by constant incidental expressions,
and by its whole structure and design that the mind of
the writer assumes that we have in the Bible a trustworthy
and authoritative expression of the mind and will of God.
The complainants have not read to understand even that
which is perfectly patent and plain, much less to mark and
inwardly digest. They have been in search for means of
attack, on a rampage for accusations. Sentences are twisted
from their connections, quoted by jumping backwards and
then forwards,[1] divorced from qualifying declarations in the
immediate context, begun with capitals by omission of important connections and obliteration of every indication that
in the book they are not thus independent. It is easy to make
a slip in citation, as experience shows, and no generous critic
will deal severely with a mere inadvertence. But where
errors are numerous, where they always favor one side, where
they are artificial, they are properly regarded as evidence of
lack of candor. That the quotations are adduced for the purpose of specification does not help the matter. They are none
the less unfair citations.

I will adduce instances in point.

The third quotation from *Progressive Orthodoxy* — com-
mencing " Even if " — begins, in the book, " *And* even if," con-
necting with a different and natural explanation of our Lord's
method of reference to the Pentateuch and Isaiah. The sixth
citation, — beginning " When we recollect "[2] — is the second member of a sentence, whose first member reads " But
the slight blemishes in the very finest optical instruments
do not prevent our obtaining from them data which to the
human mind of finest training are exceedingly exact; and

[1] pp. 231, 227, 228, 207, 208, 209, 213, 214, 221, 222. [2] Prog. Orth., p. 209.

when " etc. Half a sentence is taken, the connective omitted without indication, and the whole covered up by altering the capital letter.

The fifth quotation is followed in the paragraph from which it is taken by an antithetic sentence, beginning: "But this feature . . . is not its weakness but its strength," and by further qualification in the next paragraph in the words: "If the question mean, 'Must not such sin as still dwelt in the apostles have tinged their religious conceptions and teaching with error?' — we reply, This could not have been unless they were more under the influence of moral evil than we have any reason to suppose them to have been." That is, the answer 'Yes' is quoted and the answer 'No' omitted; and this when the negative refutes the charge of holding that the Bible is "fallible and untrustworthy even in some of its religious teachings."

The seventh quotation, — beginning, "The views of Christ," — recognizes that other ages than the apostolic have been blessed with men in whom dwelt the Spirit of wisdom and revelation. It is overlooked that before the paragraph closes allusion is made to ancient prophets, and that it is added: "No teacher in the church has ever arisen or can ever arise so filled with the Spirit as not to depend upon the apostles for conceptions of God. We can see that their situation and their exceptionally exalted life make following teachers dependent upon them as they were not dependent upon any predecessor except Christ; that their conceptions of our Lord are the framework into which all the subsequent thoughts of his church, about Him and his work, must be set; and the *norm by which the teaching of the church must shape itself.*" And then the writer goes on to show that this follows "necessarily" from their historical relation to the Incarnation; that beyond this intimate personal acquaintance with the "Word of life," there was added "the inner revelation" and "*pre-eminent endowment of the Spirit;*" that the hope even must be excluded of other teachers arising superior to them; that their conditions of spiritual endowment were "absolutely unique;" that the greatest thinkers of the church have never been able to correct one of their conceptions of Christ and that in them was fulfilled Christ's promise to lead them "into the whole truth." [1]

I will not go on with this exposure. These citations are wholly insufficient for their purpose. They are vitiated, first, by their irrelevancy. They fail, every one, as they stand, to prove the charge, or even to specify it. They are wholly defaulted, secondly, by being garbled. When taken in their proper connections they turn into a positive refutation of the charge — a refutation which would be repeated again and again by further citation, by passages for instance which may be found on pp. 10, 207, 214, 227, as well as on those already adduced.

The specifications show only this, that sometimes in *Progressive Orthodoxy* the word imperfection is used, or its equivalent, whereas in the Creed the adjective "perfect" is employed. But it is not thereby shown that the book affirms to be imperfect what the Creed says is perfect. The Creed affirms perfection of the Word of God contained in the Scriptures of the Old and New Testaments as a rule of faith and practice. I take no advantage, though I might on the theory of a merely literal interpretation, of the words "contained in." To me the Bible *is* the Word of God. But the perfection ascribed to it in the Creed is one of use and function. It is the only perfect guide in a religious life, "in faith and practice."

This formula did not originate with the framers of the Seminary Creed. The Westminster Standards declare Holy Scripture "to be the rule of faith and life," [2] "the only rule of faith and obedience," [3] "the only rule to direct us how we may glorify and enjoy Him." [4] And among the questions to candidates for ordination is this one: "Do you believe the Scriptures of the Old and New Testament to be the Word of God, the only infallible rule of faith and practice?" This last formula appears occasionally in local New England creeds. The founders apply the word infallible to the "revelation

---

[1] Prog. Orth., pp. 210–213.
[2] *Confession*, Art. II.
[3] *Larger Catechism*, 3.
[4] *Shorter Catechism*, 2.

which God constantly makes of Himself in his works of creation, providence and redemption." Their phrase respecting the Scriptures is, "the only perfect rule of faith and practice." It is the Westminster formula with the change of "infallible" to "perfect." But the formula is older than the Westminster Standards. It summed up the universal Protestant contention against the Roman Catholic doctrine of Scripture. The Council of Trent exalted Tradition to a place of co-ordinate authority with Scripture. The Bible was not the only rule because there was another. It was not the only perfect rule because it was not a complete rule but partial. Practically it was not even an infallible rule because it needed to be supplemented by Tradition, and to be authoritatively interpreted by the Church, and with the Bible alone as his guide a man might go astray from its insufficiency. This great controversy brought into use such expressions as I have cited from the Westminster Standards, and similar ones with which we are familiar in our local confessions. If you will look into Chillingworth's great work on "The Religion of Protestants," in which he contended for the famous maxim that the Bible alone is this religion, you will find *passim* the expressions "a perfect rule of faith,"[1] "the only rule" and also abundant evidence that their meaning is what I have just explained, viz., that Sacred Scripture is "the only perfect rule of faith and practice," because it is a complete rule, needing no supplementing by tradition, a plain rule requiring no infallible interpreter, whether church or pope, council or creed, a sure rule for whoever follows its teachings will believe and do what is acceptable to God and find eternal life. In a word the formula as expounded by this acknowledged master has a negative and positive side. It denies that other rules are necessary for men either as a co-ordinate source of religious knowledge or as an indispensable interpreter, and it affirms that Scripture can make the man of God "perfect, thoroughly furnished unto all good works."[2] Scripture is thus "the only perfect rule of faith and practice."

[1] See particularly Pt. I., c. 2. [2] 2 Tim. iii. 17.

In perfect consistency with this exposition, Chillingworth opens the door for all the liberty that a sound historical criticism requires in the investigation of the method in which the Bible became such a rule of faith. There is not an utterance cited by the complainants which is not covered in principle by his masterly statement, and when the complainants attempt to put such expressions as they quote from *Progressive Orthodoxy* and the *Review* into antagonism to the Creed they are not only ineffective, but they show their ignorance of principles which were formulated in the beginnings of Protestantism and long since settled by one of its universally recognized and foremost champions. Why, even so familiar a book as Professor Stuart's *Old Testament Canon* contains many a sentence just as much and just as little objectionable as those picked out and up by the complainants.

Let me present a few of these which have been handed to me by one of my colleagues :

In regard to drawing the line between what is abrogated in the Old Testament and what is now of divine authority and obligation he says : " The ultimate appeal, then, is to understanding and reason ; not in order to establish the *principles* in question, for Christ and his apostles have established them, but to make a discriminating and judicious use of these principles in determining what still remains in full force." (p. 386.)

All that refers to Old Testament rites and forms of worship is abrogated. "It remains now only as the *history* of what is past, not the rule of action for the present or the future." It unfolds " in what manner divine Providence has been educating the human race ; by what slow and cautious steps religion has advanced, and how utterly impossible it is for a religion that abounds in rites and forms to make much *effectual* progress anywhere, either among Jews or Gentiles ; still more impossible that it should be a religion to convert the world." (p. 391.)

So too all statutes and ordinances that pertain merely to the form of the Jewish ecclesiastical and civil state. (pp. 404–405.)

"Rarely will one find any considerable portion of the Old Testament where there is nothing in it of the *local* and *temporal* that must be abstracted, in order for us to reduce it to practice." (p. 404.)

The devotional psalms, "the Psalms of complaint, of thanksgiving, of imprecation, and others, all have something which savors of time and place and circumstances. These we must omit, excepting that in the *exegesis* of the Psalm we must treat them as essential, but not in the practical use of it." (p. 405.)

"It is so with the Mosaic laws."

"Even the *ten commandments* are not altogether an exception to this." The reference here is to visiting iniquity to third and fourth generation, and to the promise that thy days may be long in the land.

With reference to the question what is of present practical value in the Old Testament he says: "How few [of the commentaries] have satisfied the claims of the *reason* and *understanding* of men!"

"A commentary that would give us simply what is fairly to be learned from every part of the Old Testament in respect to present duty, or as to doctrine . . . is one of the things yet to be; for I cannot think that it now is." (p. 406.)

"What can we say of those teachers who find just as full and complete a revelation in the Old Testament of every Christian doctrine, as in the New? (p. 407.) Instances Trinity, Immortality and Future State.

"We must attribute no more to the Old Testament than belongs to it. The glory of the gospel is not to be taken away and given to a mere introductory dispensation." (p. 408.)

"We should regard them (Old Testament books) in the light of a *preface* or of an *introduction* to the Gospel."

Of current abuse of Old Testament texts: "Books of such a peculiar nature as Job and Ecclesiastes, for example, are resorted to with as much confidence for *proof texts* as if they were all *preceptive* and not an account of disputes and doubts about religious matters." (p. 409.)

"The Psalms that breathe forth imprecations are appealed to by some, as justifying the spirit of vengeance under the gospel, instead of being regarded as the expression of a peculiar state of mind in the writer, and of his imperfect knowledge with regard to the full spirit of forgiveness."

He deprecates the "violence done to the understanding and to sober common sense" in exegesis, and says it "will be certain to avenge itself at last." (p. 410.)

"There are not a few persons, who seem to feel that if the Old Testament is a work of *inspiration* it must stand on the same level with the New, and be equally obligatory. There is something of truth in this, and not a little of error." (p. 413.)

"We have a *new* and a *better* Testament than the ancient. In itself it is a sufficient guide." (p. 414.)

"Of one thing I am fully persuaded, which is, that a proper use of the Old Testament will be made in all cases, by no one who cleaves to the notion, that because the Hebrew Scriptures were inspired they are therefore *absolutely* perfect. Such perfection belongs not to a prefatory or merely introductory dispensation. It is only a *relative* perfection that the Old Testament can claim; and this is comprised in the fact, that it answered the end for which it was given. It was given to the world, or to the Jewish nation, in its *minority*." (p. 415.)

"With the exception of such sins as were highly dishonorable to God and injurious to the welfare of men, the rules of duty were not in all cases strictly drawn."

"The Old Testament morality, in respect to some points of *relative* duty, is behind that of the Gospel" (p. 416).

"The Gospel is ever and always the *ultima ratio* in all matters of religion and morals. It is . . . the highest tribunal. Whatever there is in the Old Testament which falls short of this . . . is of course not obligatory on us" (p. 417.)

"The spirit of New Testament doctrine, morality, modes of worship (so far as modes are touched upon), is always to be applied to judging of our obligations to the ancient Scriptures."

"There are imperfections in the ancient system; but they are such as the nature of the case rendered necessary. They are in accordance with the principle of the slow and gradual amendment of the race of man." (p. 418.)

In arguing against Norton he emphasizes the divine origin and authority of the Hebrew Scriptures as admitted by Christ and his apostles and Christians generally and then says: "Mr. Norton has scanned Old Testament matters in the light of New Testament revelation, and then passed sentence of condemnation upon the imperfect, because it is not perfect. Is this equitable dealing? . . . Is it any satisfactory objection against this or that specific thing in the Old Testament that the New has better arranged or modified it? Is it conclusive against the history or character of David and other potentates, that they did things in war, which were common in those days, but which the Gospel and a better state of things now forbid?" (p. 419).

Particular 2. The complainants quote from the *Andover Review*, May, 1886, p. 522, but overlook the statement on p. 524:

"So long as the doctrines of universal sinfulness, of redemption and eternal life only through Jesus Christ the Saviour, who was TRUE GOD AND TRUE MAN, and the doctrine of eternal condemnation to those who do not believe on Christ, — so long as these doctrines are faithfully and generally preached we must conclude that the pulpit which is orthodox in name is in the best sense orthodox in fact." See also *Progressive Orthodoxy*, pp. 22 *sqq*.

Particular 3. In the words "are not found" (quoted from *Progressive Orthodoxy*, p. 47), there is an obvious reference to what is learned from history and observation. The discussion does not concern itself with exceptional cases, but with the broad and patent fact of the moral helplessness of mankind apart from Christ.

Pages 54–56 are then cited; but the extract opens, if we interpret aright the reference, with the declaration:

"But Christ's power to represent or be substituted for man is always to be associated with man's power to repent. The possibility of redeeming man lies in the fact that although he is by act and inheritance a sinner, yet under the appropriate influences he is *capable* of repenting. The power of repentance remains, and to this power the gospel addresses itself." "It is to this power that Christ, the holy and the merciful, attaches himself." "Now the power of repentance, which, so far as it exists, is the power of recuperation, is superior to the necessities of past wrong-doing and of present habit." (p. 55.)

It is indeed stated that "Man left to himself cannot have a repentance which sets him free from sin and death," and that the race, without Christ, "would be hopelessly destitute of" the requisite "powers for repentance and holiness." But here the writer is evidently contemplating a radical and complete restoration of men to sonship and freedom. Compare Paul's account of his own experience in the seventh of Romans, and these words in Ephesians ii. 11, 12, "Wherefore remember, that aforetime ye, the Gentiles in the flesh, . . . were at that time separate from Christ, having no hope and without God in the world."

With the language quoted from p. 58, compare what is said on pp. 59 and 60: "Christ brings God the Person to man the person, and in such manner that God is known as the God of holy love, the loving and holy Father. The goodness of God leads men to repentance." "Or reversing the order and advancing to the ultimate fact that redemption originates with God, we may say that man is the penitent and obedient man because God in Christ is the reconciling and forgiving God." The discussion deals with the great facts of human recovery from sin. The distinction between natural ability and moral inability is important; but the original Hopkinsians never thought of putting the stress upon it which some later theologians have laid. Of one of these it was said, when the remark was made that he claimed to represent the Hopkinsians, 'Yes, with this difference: they exalted divine efficiency; he, human efficiency.' The writer of the article in *Progressive Orthodoxy* seeks to apprehend the real saving powers in the cross of Christ. His critics appear to be fumbling over the distinction of natural and moral ability.

Following their usual method, these complainants next turn back a few pages and pick up a sentence on p. 55, and, as is not unusual with them, overlook other sentences on the same page which ought to have entirely relieved their distress. We need not quote over again what has just been presented. Finally the sentence is taken from p. 126; "Where in the realm of natural law, can the Spirit find material or motive fitted to this most difficult of all tasks — the convincement of sin?" As this is a question we might wait perhaps for the complainants to answer it. Any contribution they may thus make to Christian theology will be cordially welcomed. Agassiz seems to have doubted whether nature alone gives "any very clear mark of the *character* of the Creator."[1] But this is not the point to be

[1] See Allen's Our Liberal Movement in Theology, p. 157.

here discussed. What is there in all that is adduced which shows any contrariety of opinion to the statements of the Creed? Man's natural powers of moral agency are not denied, but asserted. It is everywhere assumed that men are responsible for their sins. The discussion of the book relates to a different question, namely, How is man saved? The following extract from the early pages of the article on *The Atonement*, from which nearly all the specifications are taken, sufficiently shows this:

"Now the message of the gospel unquestionably is that man is not bound under ethical in the sense in which he is bound under physical necessity; that forces are available for the moral and spiritual life by which man can be delivered from the worst consequences of sin, and can become a new creature. Transformation may be rapid and complete. Man may be translated from the dominion of merciless necessity into the life of freedom and love. The new and higher force is the revelation of God in Christ, through which the power of sin is broken and the penalty of sin remitted. If all this is true, the gospel gains a profounder meaning than it has ever yielded before. The church comes now to man, well aware that he cannot be separated from custom, habit, heredity, fixedness of character, the social organism of which he is part. It is seen that redemption must be grounded in reason, and must meet the actual conditions of life and character and society. Atonement must express and reveal God as the supreme Reason and perfect Righteousness, who cannot deny himself, and who cannot disregard nor annul the moral law which is established in truth and right. Christian thought, having established itself on the intrinsic, absolute right and on the inexorableness of law so firmly that these may be accepted as postulates in all the inquiry, agreeing so far forth with Anselm on the one hand and with the latest natural ethics on the other, is going forward now to learn if any ethical ends are secured by the revelation of God in Christ, and secured in such a way that God energizes in man and society for a moral transformation so radical and complete that it may be called salvation, redemption, eternal life, divine sonship. . . .

"This is the question to-day concerning atonement, — What moral and spiritual ends are secured by the sacrificial life and death of Christ? How does God's attitude towards man change, and man's attitude towards God change, so that there is sufficient power for the transformation of ethical and spiritual life as against the tendencies of moral corruption? Evidently the result is of a kind that cannot be brought about by sheer omnipotence, but only, if at all, by truth and love. Thought must move in the spiritual, not in the physical realm."

We add without comment a few sentences which show the point of view and the care exercised to suggest necessary qualifications.

"Regeneration thus acquires a large and an exact meaning under Christianity. We would not deny the existence of regenerate life outside Christianity. . . . If we say the least, we can say no less than that when we pass beyond the method of the conscious renewal of the spiritual life in Christ, we pass at once into what is exceptional, vague, and indeterminate. (pp. 127, 128.)

"The moral and spiritual recovery of mankind even as an aim of benevolent purpose, presupposes the provision of a power in motive, and a use of this power proportionate to the evil to be confronted, and the good to be accomplished. 'It was the good pleasure of the Father that in Him should all the fullness dwell.' The fullness was set over against the need. Christianity is not a matter of words, but of deed and of power. Whatever we may think of antecedent revelation the apostle teaches us the large fact and truth in the case when he says, even of the days of Jesus' earthly ministry, 'The Spirit was not yet given, for Jesus was not yet glorified.'" (p. 121.)

The Creed affirms "that every man is personally depraved;" "that being morally incapable of recovering the image of his Creator, which was lost in Adam, every man is justly exposed to eternal damnation ; so that, except a man be born again, he cannot see the Kingdom of God;" "that . . . the Son of God, and He alone, by his suffering and death, has made atonement for the sins of all men;" "that the righteousness of Christ is the only ground of a sinner's justification ; that this righteousness is received through faith;" "that regeneration and sanctification are effects of the creating and renewing agency of the Holy Spirit;" . . . "that the ordinary means by which these benefits [of redemption] are communicated to us, are the word, sacraments, and prayer;" "that God's decrees perfectly consist with human liberty;" "that man has understanding and corporeal strength to do all that God requires of him; so that nothing, but the sinner's aversion to holiness, prevents his salvation."

Progressive Orthodoxy recognizes man's responsibility for his sins, affirms his moral ruin, and emphasizes the righteousness which is by faith in Christ and the renewing work of the Spirit. I am unable to see wherein this book fails to conserve the principles enunciated in the Creed on these topics. They seem to me to gain a new depth of meaning and a higher degree of reasonableness from the fact that the authors give to the universality of the Atonement and to the Incarnation the primary and central place in theology. Man's moral agency becomes the activity of a child of God, and sovereignty blends with fatherhood. The reality and guilt of sin grow darker, as the way of escape grows brighter. I do not the less accept the principles of moral agency contained in articles of the Creed which I have cited because they become more profound and far-reaching by reason of a doctrine which the Creed also contains, though without indicating its power of illumination; I refer to the article on the universality of the Atonement. If the Eternal Son became Man and died for all whose nature He made his own, then moral agency, in a world or age in which this is the central and supreme revelation of what is divine, necessarily transcends the bounds of either a legal or imperial sovereignty. I think that the fundamental principle of *Progressive Orthodoxy* is in the Creed, and that we have a right to interpret other associated doctrines by it. I maintain also that these doctrines, so far as they are not inconsistent with this principle, are better held the more they are connected with it and systematized by it.

Particular 4. I have already, in my Reply, called attention to the way in which the quotation marked as from page 64 is made up. I have also affirmed my belief that "every man who sins *is* lost, and is in danger of being remedilessly lost." I will now simply add a few quotations, several of them lying between the two page references, 55 and 64, which are given by the complainants in connection with this particular. Their point, it will be borne in mind as I read, is, that I hold, maintain and inculcate that men are not sinners unless they have heard of Christ, or at any rate are not "in danger of being lost." On page 44 and again on page 47 sinfulness is predicated of man universally. On page 48 it is said : " The consequences of holiness and of sin cannot be set aside by the will of God. On page 54 the garbled paragraph opens, in its second sentence, with recognizing " the fact " that man " is by act and inheritance a sinner," and its concluding sentence says that "on account of Christ *man* can be delivered from *condemnation*." On the opposite page (57) we read: .. " God cannot be regardless of law nor indifferent to sin in saving man from *punishment*." On the next page it is said: " The ideal relation of God is love, but the actual relation is wrath ;" on page 60, " He who is not moved to penitence and faith by Christ is under a *greater* condemnation ;" on page 61 : " It is on account of Christ that God can forgive, on account of Christ that men are not left helpless and condemned under the necessities of unchangeable law." On page 177 the cause of missions is recognized as resting on "the postulates of universal sinfulness, universal atonement, and the indispensableness of faith." And in the concluding article of the book these postulates are re-affirmed, and it is added : We have accepted these postulates in their length and breadth. We have not reduced but rather have magnified their meaning." And yet in the face of these explicit statements we are charged with teaching that men are not sinners " save as they have received a knowledge of the historic Christ ! "

Particular 5. I do not think that I need give any additional references here, and I will merely re-affirm the reply already submitted.

Particular 6. On page 33 there is a distinct recognition that the Apostle Paul teaches the propitiatory nature of Christ's sacrifice ; and on page 48 an equally clear acceptance of the Anselmic principle of a " necessity . . . in the ethical being of God . . . which even his will cannot contradict nor supersede." ". . . God cannot be regardless of law nor indifferent to sin in saving man from punishment." When it is said, "It must be confessed, however, that it is not clear how the sufferings and death of Christ can be substituted for the punishment of sin," this is not a suggestion of doubt as to the fact of Atonement but a statement of the problem, and the key to the reasoning which follows. The complainants have confused two lines of approach to the subject (p. 57), and failed to observe that the familiar one, on which their own thoughts more naturally travel, is recognized but not pursued because it is so well understood. Perhaps if they would kindly endeavor to think out what is suggested by the word "realizing," in one of the closing sentences of the article from which they quote, — "In the Atonement God promised redemption for the world by realizing his holy love in the eyes of all the nations" — their apprehensions would be relieved. Will they suggest a thought or expression that more deeply penetrates into the nature of the mysterious sacrifice on Calvary than that by which it is opened to our reverent gaze as a *Realization* in the fullness of time, at the turning point of human history, through an incarnate Redeemer and for the purpose of man's redemption, of God's righteous and holy love?

And then will the complainants, in addition, please to point out what is the theory of the Atonement made binding in the Creed as a condition of a trust? Where is it found, and how is it expressed?

Particular 7. The most charitable interpretation of this accusation is, that it is a sheer blunder, a blunder however which nothing but the oppressive exigencies of this "friendly suit" could have led sensible men to commit. It appears that it was not the original intention of the complainants to file charges and specifications themselves, but when your Reverend and Honorable Body decided that, if they thought the matter presented by them so serious as to require investigation, they should reduce their accusations to definite form, their embarrassments became such that a civilized community will treat their mistakes with appropriate lenity. It is one thing to indulge for four years in the almost unlimited license of vague accusation permissible in the columns of religious journalism, to call men Semi-Unitarians and Semi-Universalists, and the like. But it is quite a different affair to make a specific charge and to attempt to prove it. The editorial habit, however, could not be easily resisted. A Semi-Unitarian — what is he ? He must be a Sabellian. This is particularly convenient, for the Professors at Andover promise to oppose Sabellians, and we want in a friendly way to establish a violation of solemn promises and a breach of trust. We will charge them then with holding that the Trinity is modal. But either some special urgency of timeliness in pressing the complaint, or some occult influence of superior power, or some wholly mysterious cause, required such extreme rapidity of execution, that these busy, active men, charged with so many grave responsibilities, found no time to look up in their Seminary note-books or some familiar text-book what is the exact meaning of the words " modal and monarchian," as applied to the Trinity. They were caught by the word " mode," just as before they had been, when dealing with the Scriptures, with the word "perfect." The Creed says the Bible is a perfect rule, the Professors talk of imperfections. The Creed condemns Sabellians. Sabellians — perhaps they remembered this much of their Seminary lore — hold to a modal Trinity. Let us look and see if these same Professors who have so trifled with Sacred Scripture are not equally guilty in respect to the Holy Trinity. Thus searching they discovered and triumphantly produced, when required so to do, in the *amended* complaint, two passages from *Progressive Orthodoxy*, each of which contains the word " mode " in application to a Person of the Trinity. Here surely is set forth a modal Trinity, and a modal Trinity is Sabellian ! *Quid obstat?* But I respectfully submit, Mr. President and Gentlemen, this question to your decision, whether any tyro in theology could not have told these men that the distinction between a modal or real Trinity is conveyed by the use of the phrases mode of manifestation and mode of being. He who affirms the latter predicate of a distinction in the Godhead uses the formula than which no other is more firmly established in Christian Theology as the best word to discriminate the church doctrine from every form of Monarchianism. And this precise formula, or its equivalent, is the one twice employed by the writer in *Progressive Orthodoxy* whose sentences are quoted to prove that I hold to a modal Trinity. It is as absurd as an attempt to prove that President Lincoln was a believer in absolute monarchy because he used the word government when he spoke at Gettysburg of government by the people.

The phrases I have used are, in the first passage cited, "the divine nature as possessed by the Logos, or in that mode which characterizes his existence." You have there all the most characteristic forms of speech by which the Church doctrine of the Trinity has been expressed for fifteen centuries. The Logos possesses, has as his own, the divine nature. He possesses it, however, in a peculiar way or mode. This mode of possession characterizes his being. It is his personal property as the Larger Catechism says, — *his* characteristic. In the next quotation the phrase employed is, "a particular mode of the divine being," not, you observe, mode of manifestation, or relationship *ad extra*.

I think I need not stop to discuss the question of the meaning of the word "Person" as applied to the Holy Trinity. When the article quoted from, referring to the three distinctions, or modes of being, in the godhead, affirms that "Neither in itself is a Person," it uses the word Person as employed when we speak of the one absolute Person, God. I hold, and the writer of the article, judging by his language, agrees with me in holding, that each distinction is personal, but that each is a Person, (in the ordinary sense of personality, and as this idea finds its supreme realization in the Infinite and Absolute One), only in, with and through the other distinctions and as possessing the one divine nature. And the orthodoxy of this position can easily be established by the most approved writers. A doctrine antagonistic to this, and at the same time admitting personal distinctions, is sheer Tritheism, not Trinitarianism.

I will subjoin a few quotations from authors of acknowledged standing and ability, which I have taken almost at random.

Dr. Shedd teaches that the word Person, as applied to the Trinity, designates a species of existence "anomalous," "unique," "totally *sui generis*." [1]

Dr. Schaff explains the doctrine established by the great Councils thus:

"In this one divine essence there are three *persons*, or, to use a better term, *hypostases*, that is three different modes of subsistence of the one same undivided and indivisible whole. . . . Here the orthodox doctrine forsook Sabellianism or modalism which, it is true, made Father, Son, and Spirit strictly co-ordinate, but only as different denominations and forms of manifestation of the one God." [2]

In 1819 Professor Moses Stuart, in his "Letters to the Rev. William E. Channing," gave this representation of the views of Trinitarians:

"The common language of the Trinitarian Symbols is, '*That there are three* PERSONS *in the Godhead.*' In your comments upon this, you have all along explained the word *person*, just as though it were a given point, that we use this word here, in its *ordinary* acceptation as applied to *men*. But can you satisfy yourself that this is doing us justice? What fact is plainer from Church History, than that the word *person* was introduced into the creeds of ancient times, merely as a term which would express the disagreement of Christians in general, with the reputed errors of the Sabellians, and others of similar sentiments, who denied the existence of any *real distinction* in the Godhead, and asserted that Father, Son, and Holy Ghost were merely *attributes* of God, or the names of different ways in which he revealed himself to mankind, or of different relations which he bore to them, and in which he acted? The Nicene Fathers meant to deny the correctness of this statement, when they used the word *person*. They designed to imply by it, that there was some *real*, not merely *nominal* distinction in

---

[1] *History of Christian Doctrine*, I. 365.
[2] *History of the Christian Church*, III. 675.

the Godhead; and that something more than a diversity of relation or action, in respect to us, was intended. They used the word *person*, because they supposed it approximated nearer to expressing the existence of a *real distinction*, than any other which they could choose. Most certainly neither they, nor any intelligent Trinitarian, could use this term, in such a latitude as you represent us as doing, and as you attach to it. We profess to use it merely from the poverty of language; merely to designate our belief of a real distinction in the Godhead; and NOT to describe independent, conscious beings, possessing *separate* and *equal essences*, and *perfections*. Why should we be obliged so often to explain ourselves on this point? . . . I could heartily wish, indeed, that the word *person* never had come into the Symbols of the Churches, because it has been the occasion of so much unnecessary dispute and difficulty." [1]

John Calvin, in his *Institutes*, remarks as follows:—

"The Latins having used the word *Persona* to express the same thing as the Greek ὑπόστασις, it betrays excessive fastidiousness and even perverseness to quarrel with the term. The most literal translation would be *subsistence*. Many have used *substance* in the same sense. Nor, indeed, was the use of the term Person confined to the Latin Church. For the Greek Church, in like manner, perhaps, for the purpose of testifying their consent, have taught that there are three πρόσωπα (*aspects*) in God. All these, however, whether Greeks or Latins, though differing as to the words perfectly agreed in substance." [2]

"Where names have not been invented rashly, we must beware lest we become chargeable with arrogance and rashness in rejecting them. I wish, indeed, that such names were buried, provided all would concur in the belief that the Father, Son, and Spirit, are one God, and yet that the Son is not the Father, nor the Spirit the Son, but that each has his peculiar subsistence [*proprietate*]. I am not so minutely precise as to fight furiously for mere words." [3]

"But, if we hold, what has been already demonstrated from Scripture, that the essence of the one God, pertaining to the Father, Son and Spirit, is simple and indivisible, and again, that the Father differs in some special property from the Son, and the

---

[1] Op. cit., pp. 21-23, 2d ed., 1819.
[2] Op. cit. I. p. 148. Calv. Trans. Soc. Ed. 1845. [3] Ib. pp. 150, 151.

Son from the Spirit, the door will be shut against Arius and Sabellius, as well as the other ancient authors of error." [1]

Particular 8. Perhaps I need do no more than repeat my previous reply :

"The accusation is that I hold the work of the Holy Spirit to be 'chiefly confined to the sphere of historic Christianity;' or, as more definitely specified by the citation, with its context, that the 'efficacious,' regenerating, saving work of the Spirit is thus 'chiefly confined.' The opposite proposition would be that this work is 'chiefly confined to' paganism, or Judaism, or both. There can be no doubt which of these propositions is more accordant with the Creed, with orthodoxy, or with 'consistent' Calvinism as explained in the Creed. Substituting the words 'conducted within' for 'confined to,' and not doubting a universal work of the Spirit, I should admit the accusation."

I will only add that the subject is discussed in *Progressive Orthodoxy* in the light of history, observation and missionary experience — that is, as a question of fact. So far as we have evidence, or judged by its fruits, Christianity alone offers the requisite material in motive for the transformation of mankind into a spiritual temple and kingdom of God.

I think that this is implied in Pentecost, that it is the teaching of John vii. 39, and of much Scriptural authority besides. "Only when Jesus was glorified," is Dr. Milligan's comment on the passage in John's Gospel (Dr. Schaff's *Popular Commentary*), . . "would men receive that spiritual power which is the condition of all spiritual life."

Particular 9. I reaffirm but do not find occasion to expand my previous answer, save to add a few references to passages on pp. 56, 57, 60, and 61, where the sinner's condemnation under law is abundantly recognized.

Particular 10. I repeat my former reply, and refer also to my acceptance of the statement in the Creed that the Scriptures are the "only perfect rule of faith and practice." A reasonable being must be guided by reason, but it is the dictate of reason to submit to the word and authority of God.

[1] *Ib.* p. 173.

I believe, however, that reason is at the bottom of all things, the reason of the universal Creator and Redeemer. Therefore human reason may explore and question and hope to find more and more fully the truth. If the charge intends — which I do not allege — to cast a slur upon reason in matters of faith, I beg leave to refer to the nobler maxims of the leader of the party which had most to do with shaping the Seminary Creed. I quote from Dr. Park's Memoir of Samuel Hopkins.

"Our author's strength of character induced him to give an unusual prominence to the more difficult parts of theology, and thus it shaped his entire system. Whether his speculations be true or false, he has done a great work in promoting manly discussion, in convincing his readers that piety is something more than a blind sentimentalism, and that theology is something better than a superstitious faith. He has encouraged men to examine intricate theories, and the examination has saved them from scepticism. Hundreds have been repulsed into infidelity, by the fear of good men to encounter philosophical objections. Hopkins was too strong for such fears. He had that sterling common sense which loves to grapple with important truths, cost what they may of toil. The great problem of the existence of sin early awakened his curiosity, and moved the depths of his heart. A weaker man would have shrunk from the investigation of such a theme. But he was ready to defend all parts of what he loved to call 'a consistent Calvinism.' His readiness to encounter the hardest subjects and the sturdiest opponents, was foretokened by one of his early corporeal feats. It is reported that an insane man, stalwart and furious, was once escaping from his keepers with fearful speed; but the young divine intercepted him, and held him fast until the maniac gave up, and cried, 'Hopkins, you are my master.'

"Throughout the unpublished and published writings of Hopkins, there breathes a masculine spirit, which refuses to be satisfied by assertion instead of argument, and insists on the legitimate use of the faculties which God has given us. At the age of sixty-five, he writes to Dr. Hart: 'I ask what faith I shall have in the power of God, or what belief of any revealed truth, if I do not so far trust to my own understanding, as to think and be confident that I do understand that God has revealed certain truths, and what they are.' In his thirty-fifth year, Hopkins seized at what he deemed a tacit concession of Dr. Mayhew, that Arminianism could not be sustained by reason. He writes to Bellamy: 'I think he [Mayhew] says that which may be fairly construed as a crying down of reason, under the name of *metaphysical*, or some epithet tantamount.'' Hopkins was too vigorous to leave such a concession unnoticed. He turns the tables on his Arminian opposers, and they censure him for his argumentative style, — the very thing for which they have been censured, again and again, by their antagonists. Our stout champion says, that ' Pelagians and Arminians have been, in too many instances, treated so by their opponents, the professed Calvinists. The former have gloried in their reasoning against the latter, as unanswerable demonstration. The latter, instead of detecting the weakness, fallacy, and absurdity of the reasoning of the former, and maintaining their cause on this ground, as well they might, have endeavored to defend themselves from this weapon by bringing it into disgrace, and rejecting it under the name of *carnal, unsanctified reason*, etc. This has been so far from humbling or giving them the least conviction of their errors, that it has had a contrary effect to a very great and sensible degree. And no wonder; for this was the direct tendency of it, as it is an implicit confession that they felt themselves worsted at reasoning.' "[1]

Particular 11. It is evident from a few extracts from *Progressive Orthodoxy* to which I will immediately call attention that our views upon the subject here introduced have not been presented in the unguarded way which is here assumed to be true. What I am to read is a caveat to which marked prominence is given in the book against such a misrepresentation. In the " Introduction " pains was taken to say :

" Problems are above the horizon which are not yet clearly within the field of vision. Even their provisional and relative solution is at present impracticable. Too early an attempt to define and systematize is likely to cramp and repress inquiry, and to promote a dogmatic self-satisfaction which is a deadly foe to progress. The aim, accordingly, of the writers of these papers has been to keep clearly within the range of what is immediately necessary and practical. For the most part, a single line of

[1] *The works of Samuel Hopkins*, I. pp. 176-178.

inquiry has been followed, under the guidance of a central and vital principle of Christianity, namely, the reality of Christ's personal relation to the human race as a whole and to every member of it, — the principle of the universality of Christianity.

"This principle has been rapidly gaining of late in its power over men's thoughts and lives. It is involved in the church doctrine of the constitution of Christ's person. It is a necessary implication of our fathers' faith in the extent and intent of the Atonement. It is an indisputable teaching of sacred Scripture. It lies at the heart of all that is most heroic and self-sacrificing in the Christian life of our century. We have sought to apply this principle to the solution of questions which are now more than ever before engaging the attention of serious and devout minds. We have endeavored to follow its guidance faithfully and loyally, and whithersoever it might lead. We have trusted it wholly and practically. By the publication of this volume we submit our work to the judgment of a wider public. If we have anywhere overestimated or underestimated the validity and value of our guiding principle, we hope that this will be pointed out. Or if we have lost sight of any qualifying or limiting truth, we desire that this may be shown. On the other hand, if we have been true to a great and cardinal doctrine of our holy religion, and have developed its necessary implications and consequences, we ask that any further discussion of these conclusions should *recognize their connection with the principle from which they are derived, and their legitimacy, unless this principle is itself to be abandoned.*" [1]

On page 39 "a better understanding of the revealed central position of Christ in the universe, and of the absoluteness of Christianity," is claimed as a characteristic of the "New Theology." The presentation of the theory of future probation is prefaced by these remarks:

"At this point the discussion might terminate. The principle of judgment in accordance with which the destinies of men are determined we believe to be that which has now been defined. . . . We could stop here, but for a related question which has long perplexed and disturbed believers. It is a question as to the judgment and the destiny of those to whom the gospel is not made

[1] *Prog. Orth.*, pp. 3, 4. cf. pp. 13, 14, 16.

known while they are in the body. We must consider the discussion, then, in order to consider, as it may seem to deserve, this difficult question. It is, in our opinion, to be looked on as an appended inquiry, rather than as an essential question for theology. Still it is not wanting either in practical or speculative importance, and, at any rate, is at present much in dispute.

"B. A RELATED QUESTION.

"What is the fate of those millions to whom Christ is not made known in this life, and of those generations who lived before the advent of Christ?

"This may, perhaps, be only a temporary question. The time may come, we think *will* come, when all will hear the messages of the gospel during the earthly lifetime, and will know the gospel so thoroughly that knowledge and corresponding opportunity will be decisive. Then there will be less occasion for perplexity, as there will be no apparent exclusion from those opportunities which at present are given to only part of the great human family.

"The question we have raised is not new. Nor are any of the proposed answers new, although some of the reasoning is the outcome of a more profound thought of the gospel than has been gained in preceding periods. An instructive lesson for impressing the difficulty of our inquiry is a history of the various opinions which have been held during the Christian centuries by honored leaders and revered saints; such an historical sketch, for example, as Dean Plumptre gives in his recent book entitled, 'The Spirits in Prison.' No answer which has yet been given is entirely free from objections. Every one, unless he declines to accept any solution, has an alternative before him, and must rest in that conclusion which seems to him most nearly in accordance with the large meaning of the gospel, and which is exposed to the fewest serious objections. Certainly, any one should be slow to condemn those whose opinions on this vexed subject do not agree with his own hypothesis. There is no explicit revelation as to the destiny of those who on earth have had no knowledge of Christ. Therefore any inference that is drawn from the doctrines of the gospel, and from the interpretation of incidental allusions of Scripture, must be held with confession of some remaining ignorance on the part of the reasoner. The theory which we shall advance presently is offered under these conditions."

It is evident from these quotations that in our reply we might have met this entire charge by a simple and sheer denial. It is patent, by the book, that we do not, in the unqualified manner of the charge, make any opinion we entertain respecting future probation a central doctrine. In the strictest sense we do not treat it as a doctrine at all, but only as an inference from a doctrine or fundamental principle.

I do not wish, however, to avail myself of any refinements at this point. I claim full liberty under the Creed to hold in this matter whatever a true interpretation of Scripture, and of the "revelation which God constantly makes of Himself in his works of creation, providence and redemption," may make probable, and with a degree of faith as exactly proportionate to available evidence as I can measure; nay, I do not think I shall commit any sin against reason and Scripture and the God who speaks in Scripture and reason, nor violate any obligation under the Creed, if I allow myself to follow with a perfect trust wherever with the heart as well as with the head I can discover any traces of his holy and reconciling love.

I have not therefore in my reply availed myself of the opportunity given by the extravagance of the accusation to make a square denial of it. I have said: "In this unqualified form I do not admit that I hold, maintain and inculcate 'that there is and will be probation after death for all men who do not decisively reject Christ during the earthly life;' and that this should be emphasized, made influential, and even central in systematic theology." I have added: "God as revealed in Christ is to me central in theology. Whatever encourages hope that all men will have opportunity to be influenced by the motive of an offered Saviour is chiefly valuable in theology as a reflection of the character of God."

A theologian's duty, as well as a believer's, and indeed every man's, is primarily to God. What He is in his character and in his will concerning us, is the great, and all-absorbing question. This is emphatically a fundamental principle of "consistent Calvinism." The question about the heathen has a deep interest to us because they are men; a deeper interest because they are men for whom Christ died, each and every one; the deepest interest because they are children of the same God on whom all our personal hopes depend and in whom all our lives are lived. A question of this character is a fundamental question. Therefore when any inquiry arises which in the smallest degree whatsoever involves His character, I will not protect myself by any man's want of skill in attacking me. So far as the question of the heathen comes into the sphere of the ethical character of God and just so far as it is within even the faintest circles of light which we may discern if we will, it is a part of the one and the only central and fundamental question for every man: What is God? And I beg leave to emphasize that this is the real central question we have discussed in *Progressive Orthodoxy*, and not the mere issue about Probation.

That there may be no ambiguity as to my position because, on a question so vital, my assailants have blundered, I deny even the last part of this accusation with this measure of qualification.

The first part I deny, in my answer, by calling attention to the fact that what I hold is an inference from what appears to be evident, and is a reasonable inference, and that it seems to be implied in the universality of Christ's Person, Atonement and Judgment. This is a suggestion by example of the grounds of hope, and the method of it. I then deny that such an inference is inconsistent with any thing in the Creed.

Upon this basis there arise two questions. *First*, have the complainants shown that we "hold, maintain and inculcate" any thing more or other than what is here conceded? No evidence to this effect has been adduced, nor is there any.

Second. Is the drawing and accepting this inference such a departure from the Creed as brings me into disharmony with it, or into antagonism to it in my official service?

It devolves upon the complainants to prove such disharmony or antagonism. They must show, if they are to make out their case, that the inference in question is necessarily hostile to the Creed, that I cannot entertain it without being hostile to the same, that I cannot receive it without violating my solemn promise " to maintain and inculcate the Christian faith as expressed in the Creed, . . . so far as appertains to my office, according to the best light God shall give me, and in opposition to" various errors.

In reviewing the effort to establish such antagonism I have a right to demand from the complainants entire definiteness of statement, and conclusiveness of argument. They must show that I actually take positions in what they prove, or in what I admit, that I hold, which contravene my official obligations under the Creed and Statutes.

Under the Creed. The question is not one of contrariety to opinions commonly held when the Seminary was founded, nor even to opinions held by the Founders, but simply of antagonism to what they have prescribed in their Statutes. Professor Park has said that the Professors at Andover "are now under the safeguard of that Creed. They cannot be required to believe more than is involved or implied in it." This is a cardinal principle. Not the opinions of the Founders, but what they have prescribed or implied in their Statutes, is the standard by which the charge of "heterodoxy" is to be tested." As I have previously stated I do not hereby waive or discredit any claim that may arise from a larger interpretation of the word heterodoxy, I simply disregard it for the present discussion, meeting my opponents on their chosen ground.

Coming now to the accusation I notice (1) *that the Creed contains no explicit declaration upon the question at issue.*

It says nothing whatever about the condition of men who die without opportunity to hear the gospel, or to accept or reject an offered Saviour, in the intermediate state between death and judgment. All that it affirms about men who do not die in faith is contained in these words: "but that the wicked will awake to shame and everlasting contempt and with devils be plunged into the lake that burneth with fire and brimstone forever and ever."

This is Biblical phraseology. It is the only instance in the entire Creed (with one possible exception which would confirm my argument) in which such a resort is made. Everywhere else the framers use their own terms, or the traditional language of the Catechism. An awe seems to come over them when they come to the awful destiny of incorrigible sinners. They will prescribe nothing themselves. Whatever their own interpretations of Scripture they will not introduce them into a Creed which they intend shall not be altered, and which they hope will endure till the end shall come. It probably never occurred to them that men would arise who would reject their doctrines as antiquated, and then claim that it is a breach of trust to follow the Scripture which they inserted in the Creed rather than to follow their opinions which they did not insert. I repeat: they simply on a subject so grave and terrible, use the phraseology of the Bible. Uninterpreted by them, left in its original form, it has the meaning of Scripture, as they quote it, and this meaning only.

I claim that this disposes conclusively, finally, of the whole question. I have no right, you have no right, to add to this Creed; to put an interpretation on this Scriptural language other than the language which is cited bears, to give it a meaning which they did not prescribe, and when they chose to leave it uninterpreted.

I know of but one qualification. It may be that a correct interpretation of the Hebrew original, whose translation in King James's version the Founders use, would make the passage less relevant than they supposed. It would not of course be fair to the Founders for any one to take an advantage of this — if such a supposition may be pardoned. For it obviously was the intention of the Founders to introduce into their Creed an article upon the final state of the wicked. They used for this purpose a passage about whose meaning they supposed there was no reasonable doubt. It is a text which in its phraseology as they accepted it plainly refers to the final resurrection. It was commonly so understood in their time, and by the best commentators with whom they were familiar. They would not have quoted it, if they had supposed it possible that it could refer to a revival of the Jewish nation under Antiochus Epiphanes, or any thing in the history of the Hebrews.

Beyond this they cannot go. They quoted what they understood to be plainly an eschatological passage, and left it wholly uninterpreted. No man has a right to go beyond this clear intent. All the language they used, as they use it, refers to the final resurrection and judgment.

This appears from an examination of it. "The wicked"—who are they? The "incorrigibly wicked at death," it has been argued. This is an addition. Besides, who are the incorrigibly wicked "at death"? The article speaks of the resurrection and final judgment. "The wicked" is the Founders' phrase, and they add no comment. It is a Biblical phrase. In the New Testament (King James's version), it is used but once with an eschatological reference. "So shall it be at the end of the world: the angels shall come forth and sever the wicked from among the just." "*At the end of the world.*" This is the point of view of the article in the Creed, and to select any other is to read into the article what this phrase does not require, and what the context excludes. The article continues: "the wicked will awake to shame and everlasting contempt," quoting the language of the prophet Daniel, which was understood to refer to the general resurrection at the end of the world, "and with devils be plunged into the lake that burneth with fire and brimstone for ever and ever," employing still Biblical language which describes what follows upon the final judgment.[1] There is in all this no allusion and no hint of an allusion to what ensues at death in the case of men who have not heard the Gospel, nor had opportunity to learn of a Saviour. Not a syllable. All reference to such a subject here is something added to the Creed, and is wholly without warrant or authority.

The case cannot be made stronger, but it is noteworthy that, as we should expect, such a necessary construction of the language harmonizes with the context.

The state of believers is considered at three stages,—in this life, at death, and at the resurrection. The state of unbelievers is considered at but one,—the final outcome of

---

[1] Rev. xxi. 8 ; and perhaps Matt. xxv. 4.

their wickedness. The Shorter Catechism which is here followed so closely says nothing about the destiny of the wicked. The framers of the Creed were led by it through the three stages in the history of believers. They added something as to the final state of unbelievers. They had been brought to the final state of the righteous. They put in sharp contrast with this, and in Biblical and in part figurative language, the final state of the wicked. No one can rightfully add to their work as a condition of their trust.

2. *The Creed contains no implicit declaration adverse to the tenet that those who have had no opportunity to learn of a Saviour in this life may be granted such opportunity in the other life.*

It is contended that such an adverse conclusion may be deduced from the statement that "they who are effectually called do in this life partake of justification, adoption, and sanctification, and the several benefits which do either accompany or flow from them." This language, it is argued, implies that all who are saved are saved in this life. Consequently none can be supposed to have an opportunity of salvation beyond this life.

This is an attempt to find in the Creed a doctrine which is not taught in the place where it properly belongs. In an instrument so carefully drawn as the Creed, so well arranged, so studiously elaborated, such an endeavor is open to suspicion. The presumptions are against an incidental deliverance upon a question which, if the intention had been to pronounce upon it at all, would have certainly received the same pains-taking treatment which is everywhere else evinced. The character of the men who made the Creed and the character of the document are strongly adverse to the supposition that there was any purpose in this article to settle an important doctrine of eschatology. Such indirection is not the method of the Creed, nor is it the method of the men who composed it, nor of the theology of their time. In general, an incidental clause found in an article concerning one doctrine, ought to be inevitable and irresistible in its inference in order to make it equivalent to a direct statement which is wholly absent when and where it properly belongs.

It is further to be noticed that the object of the article cited is not to affirm, nor does it assert, that the effectually called are called in this life. This may be implied, but the purpose of the article is to state that certain blessings come in this life to the effectually called. The obvious purpose of the article therefore is not friendly to the supposition that it was intended to decide a wholly different question, namely whether some persons may be effectually called and saved in another life.

This brings to view another difficulty. The article before us does not deal with the number of the elect, or make any statement or involve any implication on this subject. Its purpose is not to define or determine who are effectually called, but simply to assure believers that the gospel has for them great and heavenly blessings which they may partake of in this life of conflict and toil. It is forcing language written for such a use to make it serve as the statement of a dogma respecting the question what opportunities may exist for the implantation and beginning of saving faith. The article is written for Christian believers. It is taken directly from the Shorter Catechism. It deals solely with believers, and presupposes their existence. The heathen are no more within its view than the angels. It is a violation of the accepted canons of interpretation to make it cover and decide questions of a different order, relating to a different class.

I think these considerations are sufficient of themselves to warrant the rejection of this method of proof. We are not, however, merely *warranted* in thus discarding it. A careful and thorough examination of the article leads to conclusions which absolutely require such a result. For it becomes evident that the interpretation I am opposing not merely forces the meaning of the article but makes it contradictory to the Standards of which its original formed a part, and puts it out of harmony with the Creed to which it has been transferred.

The article, as I have stated, is simply appropriated from the Shorter Catechism. Unless there is some decisive reason to the contrary it must bear the meaning as transferred which it has in its original appearance. Any interpretation which it is impossible to give to it as first written certainly cannot be necessary when it is simply repeated; and when, in addition, we find that the same impossibility also appears in its new connection, we are compelled wholly to reject such an explanation.

It will perhaps make my argument more clear if I first reduce the reasoning I am opposing to the syllogistic form, and then show where it fails. It may be stated thus:

The effectually called are the elect.
The effectually called receive salvation in this life.
Therefore the elect receive salvation in this life.

The elect are saved in this life.
None but the elect are saved.
Therefore none are saved except in this life.

This reasoning confuses certain specified blessings of salvation with the beginning or principle of salvation. But letting this pass it is valid only in case the minor premise of the first syllogism must mean: All the effectually called receive salvation in this life. But this indispensable extension of the minor premise is impossible on any just principles of interpretation of either the Catechism or the Creed, and therefore the reasoning breaks down. For if there may be some who are effectually called, and therefore are of the elect and therefore will be saved, who do not receive this salvation here they must be saved elsewhere; which is precisely the hope of *Progressive Orthodoxy*.

The Westminster Standards affirm that "elect infants, dying in infancy, are regenerated and saved by Christ through the Spirit, who worketh when, where, and how He pleaseth. So also are all other elect persons who are incapable of being outwardly called by the ministry of the word."

Now if the "effectually called," in the article quoted from the Catechism and adopted into the Creed, include all the elect, then we must hold that elect infants receive in this life the blessings which are enumerated, and so also must all other elect persons who are incapable of hearing the gospel. What now are these blessings? The article before us enumerates them in part. They are "justification, adoption, and sanctification and the several benefits which do either accompany or flow from them." In the Shorter Catechism these "benefits" are explained to be "assurance of God's love, joy in the Holy Ghost, increase of grace and perseverance therein to the end."

If, then, the effectually called referred to in the article under consideration embrace all the elect, and, as is expressly stated, there are "elect infants" and elect "other persons" who never are "outwardly called by the ministry of the word," it follows that all these infants who die in infancy, and these other persons who never hear the gospel, receive in this life the blessings included in justification, adoption and sanctification, and the other benefits described;—that is, they experience in this life 'conviction of sin, enlightenment in the knowledge of Christ, renewal of will, the Spirit's persuasion and power to embrace Jesus Christ freely offered in the gospel, pardon and acceptance as righteous in God's sight, the imputation of Christ's righteousness which is received by faith alone, reception into the number and admission to all the privileges of the sons of God, ability more and more to die unto sin and live unto righteousness, assurance of God's love, peace of conscience, joy in the Holy Ghost, increase of grace and perseverance therein to the end.' Blessed infants! But who in his senses can think of putting an interpretation on this article which commits it to such absurdities?

We are still however far from being through with these consequences. For there is another alternative. If the "effectually called" in the article before us are all the elect, and all the elect consequently receive all these blessings in this life, it follows that only those are effectually called to whom such a description applies. Now it is impossible to apply it to the experience of infants and persons who know nothing of Christ. Hence we must conclude that there are no "elect infants," and no "other elect persons" beyond the reach of the Christian ministry — not a soul imprisoned here from the light which is so pleasant and the truth which is life, among the elect ; not a pagan child or woman or man, — not one elected ; and therefore all are forever lost !

The simple truth is, as I have said, that the Catechism was written for believers and their children, for Christian families and peoples. It was not composed before the Fall, or the Incarnation, nor in Africa. Torture its definitions, extort an unnatural meaning, and you make a consistent interpretation of the Westminster statements concerning effectual calling impossible.

It is important to notice that the Seminary Creed recognizes the Westminster and Savoy distinction between the ordinary means of grace and those which the Spirit may employ at his good pleasure. It thus requires for its consistent interpretation that the article respecting the benefits received in this life by the " effectually called " be not pressed beyond its original purpose and scope. Where the Creed speaks of the way in which men become " partakers of the benefits of redemption " it says : " the ordinary means by which these benefits are communicated to us are the word sacraments and prayer." The phrase " the ordinary means " is from the Westminster Standards and recalls the antithesis already noticed.

The article in the Creed connects thus with the same larger circle of thought recognized by the Westminster divines. It would be against the whole stream of history to put upon a Creed prepared in New England at the beginning of the nineteenth century as a basis of union of all phases of Calvinism, a narrower construction than that intended for the same words by theologians a century and a half earlier. The Westminster divines admitted a wider working of God's grace than they could define, and now the Andover Creed which copies their words, and at the same time teaches a universal atonement, is to be interpreted so as to shut the door which even the men who held to a limited atonement, to say the least, did not close !

And after all, supposing that the article before us were

thus perverted from its purpose, and made inconsistent with its history and the Creed, it would not then teach that the heathen can have no future opportunity of grace, but simply that they will not avail themselves of it any more than do the non-elect who have this opportunity here. And who can believe that the Founders both bungled and were irreverent in this fashion, as would be true of them if they intended to have this article construed as proposed.

A statement certainly ought to be absolutely decisive to justify an interpretation loaded with so many difficulties and even impossibilities. As it stands, so far is it from being thus conclusive that such a use of it turns it from its apparent purpose, attributes to it a design unsupported by evidence, puts it into contrariety with other declarations in the same Standards, and requires an interpretation of the Creed that makes it a condition of office at Andover to teach what never has been taught there from the beginning, namely, that all who do not hear the gospel in this life, including all infants and young children, and multitudes of the unfortunate who have lived in Christian lands without the requisite organs of mental and moral life, are not among the "effectually called," and therefore are not of the "elect," and therefore are lost forever. And such logic is to be applied to the Creed in order to squeeze out of it, if possible, what the framers of it would not write in it when they composed the article respecting the doom of the wicked.

Besides this inferential argument, I know of but one other which is employed in order to render it impossible for a Professor at Andover to hope that a universal gospel may have some provision of mercy for the millions upon millions who do not hear of it in this life.

It has been supposed that the Founders defined pretty clearly in their Creed the doctrinal test which they desired to impose. Until very lately no other has been so much as suggested. But the same ingenuity which has extracted a modal Trinity out of phraseology which used the long established and technical nomenclature of an ontological Trinity, and which has treated the articles of *Progressive Orthodoxy* as though they were a bushel of words out of which children might construct sentences to suit themselves, has discovered in the Statutes a new Creed. We have had before disputes over the Original Founders' Declaration, and the Creed of the Associate Founders; but now there appears a third one, never before known, nor suspected. Certainly these Statutes are progressive, if Orthodoxy is not. This new Creed is discovered in the Preamble to the Statutes.

In the deeply interesting, and I may say affecting, Preamble to the Statutes of the Associate Foundation, the Associate Founders mention some of the motives which led them to consecrate their gifts to the purpose of "increasing the number of learned and able Defenders of the Gospel of Christ, as well as of orthodox, pious, and zealous Ministers of the New Testament." Among these considerations they mention the fatal effects of the apostasy of man without a Saviour, the merciful object of the Son of God in assuming our nature and dying for our salvation, the institution of the Christian ministry, and the fact that " notwithstanding this appointment the greatest part of the human race is still perishing for lack of vision." These latter words have been seized upon and turned into an article of faith and a condition of the trust which has been instituted.

Such a use of them when explained will strike every candid mind as illegitimate. They are not a part of any declaration, creed or promise which these men saw fit to require of those to whom they committed their trust. They are simply declarations of a motive by which they were actuated in making their gift, to be respected as such, to be regarded so far as they express a permanent law and motive of Christian conduct, but not to be exalted to a position which the Founders themselves did not assign them; viz., that of a required article of faith.

I say this chiefly as a protest against the method of this argument of the complainants, rather than against its matter. For I " hold, maintain and inculcate," as my own belief and as a motive in life, that men are perishing for lack of vision, i.e., for the want of a knowledge of the gospel. Every sinner is perishing, and is in danger of perishing everlastingly, and will thus perish save as redeemed by Christ. Paul, as a friend has suggested, goes so far as to say, "For as many as have sinned without law, shall also perish without law." This is stronger language than that of the Founders. I submit to the Apostle. But how would Paul, were he on the earth, rebuke men who still persist, after the clearest demonstration that such was not his teaching, in claiming that his words compel us to hold that all the heathen actually perish, that not one will be saved. He believed that men were perishing for lack of vision, but not that this exhausted the divine purpose concerning them. Many of them did not perish, for through this same Apostle they heard of Christ, and believed in Him. Multitudes now are perishing, but whether everlastingly or not, depends on something not taken into account when such language is used.

It states the truth, but not the whole truth. It presents a motive which every Professor at Andover should be governed by, but it is not a statement of a doctrine which rules out all hope for the heathen, any more than does Paul's stronger declaration, "As many as have sinned without law shall also perish without law," for to some of such he afterwards wrote the letter known as the Epistle to the Ephesians, with its glowing representation of the revealed mystery, and its assurance that '*the dead in trespasses and sins, without Christ, having no hope, without God in the world, now had access by one Spirit unto the Father, and had become a habitation of God through the Spirit.*'

There is one other consideration, or class of considerations, to which I would invite your special attention before I leave this particular numbered eleven.

In the reply which I filed Nov. 30, referring to "opportunity to be influenced by the motive of an offered Saviour," the remark is made: "It seems to be implied in the universality of Christ's Person, Atonement, and Judgment." In *Progressive Orthodoxy*, this universality is often spoken of as a principle, "the reality of Christ's personal relation to the human race as a whole, and to every member of it, —

the principle of the universality of Christianity." This principle is put forward as the key to the whole volume (pp. 3, 4).

What I wish now to submit to you is, that this principle is covered, and, I may say, is made prominent in the Creed.

The Creed affirms the Deity of Christ and his Eternal Sonship. This Eternal Son became man and continues to be God and Man in two distinct natures and one person forever. This is as distinct a doctrine as words can contain of the universality of Christ's Person in its constitution. He is God, — you cannot limit his relation, therefore, without circumscribing his divinity. I speak not now of limitation in method of revelation, but in nature or essence. He is man, but so that his manhood unites in one person with the Eternal Son; he is not an individual member of the race, therefore, like you and me, but its universal head. Now take a step forward with the Creed: "[I believe] that, agreeably to the covenant of redemption, the Son of God, and he alone, by his suffering and death, has made atonement for the sins of all men." I shall endeavor to show further on that here we have one of the two distinctive notes of this Creed, that if anything in the Creed must be taken with absolute literalness and in the full force of its language, this *a fortiori* must be. It is enough now to leave it with this repetition of its words, *Agreeably to the covenant of redemption, the Son of God, and He alone, by his suffering and death, has made atonement for the sins of all men.*

Now the inference which my associates and myself have drawn in the volume called *Progressive Orthodoxy*, is to our view a legitimate and even necessary deduction from the principle thus emphasized in the Creed. So far were we from supposing that we were teaching contrary to the Creed, that we regarded ourselves as developing one of its most characteristic principles, namely that of the universality of the religion of the cross of Christ. We were fortified in this conviction by the fact that there is another principle in the Creed which also aids to our conclusion. It, too, as I will subsequently try to show, is a characteristic, a special note and feature of the Creed. I refer to the principle that God's government of mankind deals with men as free moral agents, that sin and righteousness are not transferable quantities or qualities, nor passive states, but imply always personal agency. God deals not only with man, but with men, every man, and deals with each as a free moral agent. Put this and that together and grant the universality of Christianity, and that every man is dealt with in accordance with this universality as a free moral agent, and we have the entire premise of our argument. And this premise is not only in the Creed, but is there as its most distinctive feature.

I suppose no one will question that we have a right to the logic of the Creed. If a conclusion thus obtained contradicts some statement elsewhere made in the same document, a question of interpretation arises. But I need not stop to discuss this question here, for the Creed makes no statement inconsistent with our inference. We have a right, therefore, to our conclusion so far as the Creed is concerned. That, at any rate, does not estop us. It is not a condition of the trust we have received that no such inference be drawn, even if the inference be incorrect. The Founders have imposed upon your Reverend and Honorable Body serious responsibilities, but I think you will not regret that you are not made responsible for every instance of bad logic on the part of each Andover Professor.

I know not that I need weary you with any detailed reply to the remaining particulars in the Amended Complaint. I seem to myself to have said all that is necessary concerning them in the Reply which has been filed.

I think, also, that I have now covered the ground which has been definitely chosen for the present issue by the complainants. Everything else which they have introduced is not sufficiently specific and plain as an accusation to enable and require me to answer it.

I claim therefore that upon every one of the charges which are properly in issue the complainants have failed to show that I "hold, maintain and inculcate" in my office as Professor anything not in harmony with or antagonistic to the Creed and Statutes of the Seminary, and that I am therefore entitled to a complete acquittal. And here I might safely, I doubt not, rest my case.

But I ask your indulgence in the peculiar position in which I am placed, in submitting some further considerations, strictly relevant, as I conceive, to the preceding issue, but derived from a broader range of views than has been possible in following one by one particular accusations.

The official pledges and promises at Andover do not require the Professors to think and teach in all respects alike. They do, however, make it imperative that we should open and explain the Scriptures to our pupils with integrity and faithfulness. They impose upon us the sacred obligation to unfold the truths of the Creed in opposition to past heresies and current errors which are hazardous to men, *according to the best light God shall give us.* This is a law for the conscience of every Professor.

This I have promised. How am I to keep this promise? This inquiry involves these practical questions. How am I to accept the Creed of the Seminary? How ought I to accept it? How ought you to require me to accept it?

I raise deliberately this larger question, with all that it includes. I should have been glad, if instead of compelling me to wander through the long and tedious list of preposterous charges which I have reviewed, the complainants had raised directly the vital issue, although it is perhaps creditable to their sagacity that they have not.

I maintain — you will pardon me if, under the conviction of the utter unreasonableness of the attack which has been made upon our fidelity and our liberties, I do maintain — that we are entitled at your hands to something more than a technical acquittal. We have endeavored, in sincerity and good conscience, to put our Lord's money out to usury. It has well been said that if there are perils in such a course there are greater perils in the opposite course. The man who buried his talent was very faithful and very conservative, as some men understand fidelity and conservatism, but our Lord applied to him other designations. We have received the Creed of the Seminary as a sacred trust. We have sought to put its truths out to usury. No man, in my humble judgment, really takes the Creed of the Seminary, no man is fit to be a teacher of young men on its foundations, who does not thus endeavor. It has been said that eventually there will be two sets of Professors at Andover; one who will take the Creed and do little else, another that will give the lectures. I may be wrong, but I have not supposed this to be the " true intention " of the Founders.

Permit me then to state the principles by which I have been governed in my acceptance and use of the Creed, that is, in fulfilling my promise to maintain and inculcate the Christian faith as expressed in the Creed . . . "so far as may appertain to my office, according to the best light God shall give me . . ."

1. *I accept the Creed as it is written.* I have supposed my first duty to be to understand what it says, to gather its meaning from its own words, interpreting them by the ordinary and established rules of interpretation. With this understanding of the formula I take the Creed literally. I reject as dishonest the theories of creed-subscription designated by the phrases " private interpretation," " non-natural sense."

2. I accept the Creed *in the outcome and completeness of its meaning when compared part with part.* I do not find its meaning in one article alone, for there are, besides the Declaration, thirty-six distinct articles. I subscribe not merely to the words of the Creed, but rather to the meaning which the words yield when part is compared with part, article with article, clause with clause. Occasionally a single technical word may modify an entire article, as the word " constituted " which may be understood to contain a theory going back to the Council of Trent and into the scholastic disputes between the followers of Aquinas and those of Duns Scotus, or the word " Person " in the article on the Trinity, which has a history from the days of Tertullian; or the

word "personally" in the article on Depravity, which has in it the outcome of disputes between different schools of Calvinism, as well as between Calvinists and Arminians, which had been going on for centuries.

Whatever is the outcome of the Creed as a whole I accept.

An opposite, or apparently opposite theory of subscription has been asserted with great positiveness and argued with much force. It is that a Professor in signing the Creed accepts each article by itself. I admit the obligation to believe in every doctrine of the Creed, and to an acceptance of every article as it forms a consistent part of the whole; but I deny the binding force of each individual statement, taken apart from other statements. It is said: You affirm your belief in each. My reply is, that I cannot be required to believe in contradictions, and that the Creed must be allowed to interpret itself. I cannot suppose that in the same breath the Founders intended to require me to be a "consistent" Calvinist and to take an inconsistent Creed. They must therefore have intended to give me liberty of interpretation as respects particular articles.

Let me make this clear by an example. When the Creed comes to the topic of Redemption it takes three articles in succession from the Catechism and adds a fourth original to itself. The articles read: —

"[I believe] that God of his mere good pleasure from all eternity elected some to everlasting life, and that he entered into a covenant of grace to deliver them out of this state of sin and misery by a Redeemer; that the only Redeemer of the elect is the eternal Son of God, who for this purpose became man, and continues to be God and man in two distinct natures and one person forever; That Christ, as our Redeemer, executeth the office of a Prophet, Priest and King; that agreeably to the covenant of redemption, the Son of God, and He alone, by His suffering and death, has made atonement for the sins of all men."

Down to these last words we have the language, *the ipsissima verba*, of the Catechism. And even in this article we have the traditional formula "covenant of redemption."

Now if you take these articles, each as it stands, giving to each its natural, historical, full meaning, you are involved in an insoluble contradiction of belief. The first three articles state in unequivocal terms the doctrine of limited atonement: the fourth expresses plainly the doctrine of universal atonement. In other parts of the Creed it is claimed that phraseology is employed broad enough to admit the theories of all parties to the coalition, the Old or High Calvinists, the Moderate Calvinists, and the Hopkinsian Calvinists. However this may be, here, at least, the first party completely surrendered. It is just possible that if he had chosen so to do a High Calvinist might have said "made atonement for" means "sufficient for" and nothing more, but this puts a strain upon the words. They signified much more than this to the Hopkinsians. They meant more to the first Professor of Christian Theology at Andover, who received his nomination to their chair from the so-called Original Founders, as appears from his celebrated missionary sermon at Salem in 1812, in which he emphasizes the motive of an atonement not only "sufficient for Asiatics and Africans," but "made for them as well as for us." We may not doubt that they were understood in their evangelical sense by Moderate Calvinists who aided in the counsels from which the Seminary originated. Perhaps I spoke too strongly when I used of any Calvinist who had a part in the construction or institution of the Creed the word "surrendered"; there may have been no resistance, no disagreement at this point, though the earlier Calvinists of New England, represented by Samuel Willard, spurned even the concession that Christ's death was "sufficient" for all.

We have thus in the Creed new language, expressing what was still a novelty in Calvinistic doctrine, the truth that Christ on the cross died for all men, thrust into immediate sequence upon the established and traditional formulas which had affirmed for nearly all the preceding generations in New England that He died for the elect only. I say *only*, for though this word does not occur in these formulas, its meaning is indelibly impressed on them. It is there by the technical and well-understood use of terms, there emphatically by the necessary connection and logic of the chosen articles, there unmistakably and completely. First you have the decree of election, then the covenant of grace which included the eternal covenant of Redemption between the Father and the Son and the elect in Him; then, in pursuance of this electing decree, the incarnation of the Eternal Son, who, as our Redeemer, i.e., as Redeemer of the elect, executed the office not only of Prophet and King, but of Priest, in which latter office, as the Catechism explains, and the traditional theology fully agreed, He offered " up of himself a sacrifice to satisfy divine justice and reconcile us to God," all, you notice, as Redeemer of the elect, and for the elect, and in pursuance of the decree of election. I see not how any man who takes these articles literally as they stand, who sneers at taking the Creed " in the gross," and insists on the acceptance of every doctrinal statement, can possibly extricate himself from the necessity of first saying: "I believe that Christ executeth his office of priest under the decree of election, and for the purpose of that election," and then of immediately confessing " I believe that he executeth this office of priest under a different decree and for another purpose, namely, to die for the sins of the non-elect as well as of the elect." There is, indeed, one supposable way out of the contradiction, that of assuming that the whole race is elected, or predetermined, to salvation, as Schleiermacher believed; but this is only a temporary escape, for, apart from the difficulty of interpreting the word "some" as meaning all, the closing sentences of the Creed are unfriendly to a doctrine of universal restorationism, and the subscriber would find that he had only exchanged one contradiction for another.

This antagonism in the Creed of two doctrines of the atonement might be confirmed by tracing in detail the development of the two phrases "covenant of grace " and " covenant of redemption," and of the doctrine of the order of the divine decrees, but I have said enough by way of illustration — I am satisfied that it is simply impossible to take the Creed in the way which I am opposing. I do not believe such a method ever would have been thought of but for the exigencies of controversy. There is a simple way out of these difficulties,—simple, but like many another simple principle it is found, when thoroughly applied, to be fruitful in important results. It is the path which the framers of the Creed must have intended should be followed,—*its acceptance as a whole and as it interprets itself.*

3. *I accept the Creed for substance of doctrine.* I employ this phrase under certain very careful restrictions. Were it not for the phrases "federal head and representative," "covenant of grace," "covenant of redemption," I should not need to use it at all, and I am not sure but that what I have said about taking the Creed as a whole comprehends whatever qualification I give to these terms. Still, for the sake of the utmost explicitness, I will state precisely what latitude I suppose this mode of taking the Creed permits. I do not understand that I am availing myself thereby of any other liberty than the framers intended should be used, or than was exercised while they were living and acting as Visitors, and than has been acknowledged and practised ever since.

The phrase "for substance of doctrine" appears in the *Preface* to the *Cambridge Platform*, adopted by the Synod of 1648. Referring to the Confession "agreed upon by the reverend assembly of divines at Westminster," the *Preface* says: "Finding the sum and substance thereof, in matters of doctrine, to express not their own judgment only, but ours also . . . we thought good to present . . . to our churches . . . our professed and hearty assent and attestation to the whole confession of faith (for substance of doctrine)." The Synod also passed unanimously a vote expressing "consent thereunto, for the substance thereof." From that early time on this method of accepting a Creed or Platform has obtained in New England. In his letters to Dr. Ware, the first Abbot Professor, enjoying the confidence of both sets of Founders of the Seminary and pre-eminent in his exertions to ensure the union, and writing only four years after a "perpetual union" was "established," remarked: "As it is one object of these Letters to make you acquainted with the real opinions of the Orthodox in New England, I would here say, with the utmost frankness, that we are not perfectly satisfied with the language used on this subject [Imputation] in the Assembly's Catechism. . . . Hence it is common for us, when we declare our assent to the Catechism, to do it with an express or implied restriction."[1] Dr. Woods subsequently modified his interpretation of the Catechism, but his testimony as to the custom and feeling of the Orthodox at that time and to his own liberty is not thereby affected. Dr. Humphrey, President of Amherst College, and a Visitor of the Seminary, once remarked, "No mortal man, with a mind of his own, ever accepted the Westminster Catechism without qualifications of his own." "He was right," adds Professor Phelps, "the same is true of every Confession, — unless it be some brief compendium of historic *fact*, rather than of *doctrine*, like the Apostles' Creed."[2] And the editor of the *Congregationalist*, between four and five years since,[3] defending himself from the imputation of hostility to creeds, especially the Andover Creed, remarked, . . . "for substance we heartily accept it, as Professors Park and Phelps have always done."

Even that stern censor of former Professors at Andover, Rev. Daniel Dana, D.D., while contending against their heresies, made this noteworthy concession: "Nor will I contend that the man who has taken a lengthened creed should be trammelled by all the *minutiæ* which it may embrace.[4] And Dr. Hodge, in the *Princeton Review*, speaking for the Old School wing of the Presbyterian Church nearly a generation ago, remarked (I use this extract on the *a fortiori* principle):

"It is a perfectly notorious fact, that there are hundreds of ministers in our Church, and that there always have been such ministers, who do not receive all the propositions contained in the Confession of Faith and Catechisms. . . . The principle that the

---

[1] *Letters to Unitarians*, Andover, 1820, p. 45.
[2] Quoted by Rev. Dr. Fiske in *The Creed of Andover Theol. Sem.*, 1882, p. 32.
[3] June 21, 1882.
[4] *Sermon on the Faith of Former Times*, 1848, note to p. 16.

adoption of the Confession of Faith implies the adoption of all the propositions therein contained . . . is impracticable . . . "is more than the vast majority of our ministers either do or can do. To make them profess to do it is a great sin. It hurts their conscience. It fosters a spirit of evasion and subterfuge. It teaches them to take creeds in a 'non-natural sense.' It at once vitiates and degrades." [1]

A common method in New England may be illustrated by an extract from the covenant of the Church in Salem, of which Dr. Daniel Hopkins, the brother of Dr. Samuel Hopkins, was pastor from 1778 to 1814, — the church, it is of further special interest to note, with which the Associate Founder John Norris attended worship.

" Professing a belief in the Christian Religion as contained in the Scriptures of the Old and New Testament, and embracing that scheme of doctrine which is exhibited in what is called The Assembly's Shorter Catechism, as expressing, for substance, those important truths which God has revealed to us in his holy word." And again: " Knowing the necessity of order and discipline in every body of fallible men, we promise to submit ourselves to the government of Christ in his church agreeably to the directions on this subject contained in the eighteenth chapter of Matthew, and as more fully set forth in the Platform of Church Discipline drawn up by the Congregational Synod, at Cambridge, New England, A.D. 1648, which, in substance, we adopt, as agreeable to the rules and spirit of the gospel." [2]

In entire concurrence with the method familiar to Dr. Hopkins and Mr. Norris at Salem, and in the line of the testimonies already adduced, are the reminiscences and testimony of the venerable Gardiner Spring, a son of Dr. Samuel Spring, one of the authors of the Seminary Creed and one of the first Visitors. He says, referring to the Westminster Confession:

" Few, in this age of inquiry, *believe every word of it.* Nor did our fathers. I myself made two exceptions to it when I was re-

---

[1] Reprinted in *Church Polity*, pp. 330-332.
[2] *The Covenant of Third Church of Christ in Salem*, Salem, 1841, pp. 6, 7, 8.

ceived into the Presbytery of New York fifty-five years ago. Nor were those exceptions any barrier to my admission.[1] I am no bigot and no friend to innovations. Let our Confession and Catechism stand. . . . Witherspoon, Rodgers, McWhorter, Smith, Miller and Richards were not men of strife, nor did they lend their influence to awaken jealousies, heart burnings, and chilling alienations among those who ought to love as brethren. We have no Act of Uniformity to compel a perfect unanimity in every minute article of so extended a Confession. There are shades of thought and forms of expression, in regard to which men will not cease to think for themselves. I could specify many points in which not a few of our ministers and ruling elders do not exactly agree with our standards. Yet they are all HONEST CALVINISTS, and receive our standards as the most unexceptionable formularies ever drawn up by uninspired men, and receive them as a whole with all their hearts. The iron bed of Procrustes is not suited to the spirit of the age. Some modern Theseus will yet be raised up, and show to the church that there is small space for the couch of bigotry in the nineteenth century.[2]"

I will add but one more testimony, and this not from a clergyman, but from a decision of the Supreme Court of Massachusetts rendered by Justice Thacher in the year 1815.

It was contended that a legacy to the Seminary was void, because " the original design of the founders of the Academy was to propagate Calvinism, as containing the important principles . . . of our holy Christian religion, as summarily expressed in the *Westminster Assembly's Shorter Catechism;* whereas, the design of the donors of the Associate Foundation is to add to *Calvinism* the distinguishing features of *Hopkinsianism*, a union or mixture inconsistent with the original design of the original founders of the Academy and of the theological institution." It was further contended, that if there were 'but one single article in the Creed contrary to Calvinism, or a single article omitted from the Creed which characterized Calvinism as understood at the time of the

---

[1] i.e. 1810. Two years after the Associate Foundation was established.
[2] *Life and Times of Gardiner Spring,* II. pp. 21, 22.

foundation of the Academy,' the legacy was null and void. The Court overruled and rejected the principle that a Creed must be taken in its several articles irrespective of other articles or equally required statements of doctrine.

It confirmed as of legal validity the principle which I have stated already under number two (2). It further urged the duty of " charity of construction," by which " technical propositions, should not be pressed, by a construction "astute, narrow and uncharitable," into an antagonism which could be avoided ; and, applying this principle, the Judge said : " For myself, I confess that I do not clearly perceive any other sense than that in which the articles mean substantially the same thing, notwithstanding some diversity of expression, in which they can be said to be true and consistent with the Christian religion."

I quote this last opinion, not merely on account of its great weight as testimony, but because it indicates the true sense and application in the case before us of the phrases "substantially" and "for substance of doctrine."

These phrases are sometimes objected to, not without reason, as vague. Dr. Hodge makes this criticism. But their convenience and utility keep them in use, and as it were compel it. Dr. Hodge, after rejecting them, gives illustration upon illustration which implies his acceptance of just what they are commonly understood to mean.

These phrases do not mean that a signature for substance of doctrine can cover a method by which the substance of a creed is elinminated ; nor one by which any doctrine is rejected which belongs to a creed when it is regarded as a whole. They cover two points : first, a distinction between the necessary, integral parts or doctrines of a creed and those which are subsidiary and non-essential ; second, a distinction between contents [substance] and form.

In the first of these two senses it may be thought that the phrases " for substance of doctrine " or " substantially " can have no place in the interpretation of a creed so precise as that appointed by the Associate Founders. Such a use, it may be feared, would run into the objectionable method by which a doctrine accepted "for substance" is "substantially" rejected. I admit the necessity of care and explicitness. I deny, however, that the phrases have no application, or are of no service. They embody the principle expressed by Justice Thacher in the words "charity of construction."

A Creed like the Andover is not the work of one mind, but of many minds; not of one age, but of very many. Its traditional phraseology is the larger part of it. It deals with many subjects which are only approximately apprehended by the Church as a whole, and are somewhat differently apprehended by various schools of thought, and various theologians, all of whom, however, are in general agreement. Take what are called the mysteries of Christianity — the Trinity, the union of two natures in one Person. The Creed of Chalcedon, which is the standard orthodox symbol on this latter mystery, is called in the records a "boundary." It is a definition in the sense of pointing out certain errors to which faith is exposed and which the true doctrine will exclude, certain limits on either side, which cannot be passed without renouncing certain necessary elements of belief. The Creed says: 'The doctrine is — there are two natures; hold this theory or that, and you deny one nature or the other, the divine or the human. The doctrine is: There is one person; hold this theory or that, and you come into contradiction to this personal unity.' But no man in his senses ever thought that this definition gives us an exhaustive statement of the doctrine of the Person of Christ, or shuts up a man who confesses it to every subsidiary formula which men have invented in endeavoring more firmly to apprehend it, or more fully to appropriate it. It lies in the nature of the truths confessed in a creed, that they are not measurable nor ponderable nor definable like the commodities or currencies of commerce, like an acre of ground, or a house-lot, or a dollar whether gold or silver. One does not sign a creed precisely as he signs a note. There is a mischievous fallaciousness in the way in which men use such comparisons, and then proceed to impeach their brethren's honesty, simply because they do not know what they themselves are talking about.

This principle of "charitable construction" by which diversities of form in holding a doctrine are overlooked, has been employed in the history of the Seminary and under the eyes of its founders, so as to cover not merely a diversity as to the form but as to the substance of subsidiary or unessential doctrine. One perfectly plain tenet of the Creed, if an individual and important phrase is to be pressed, has never been required. At one time I presume most of those who subscribed, Professors and Visitors alike, did not accept it in its proper meaning as it stands in the Creed. I refer to the doctrine of the Eternal Sonship.

The Creed says: "[I believe] that the only Redeemer of the elect is the eternal Son of God, who for this purpose became man, and continues to be God and man in two distinct natures and one person forever." Every Professor, every Visitor, since the Seminary was founded, has signed this statement. One of the earliest signatures is that of Moses Stuart. In his *Letters to Rev. William E. Channing* (" 1819, republished in five successive editions ") Prof. Stuart repudiated, as is well known, the Nicene and historical church doctrine of Eternal Generation, or that the Son was always Son. He admitted an eternal distinction in the divine nature, that this distinction became incarnate and was called Son as incarnate, but denied that the name Son properly designates this distinction considered as eternal. In a word, the words Eternal Son did not mean to him what they had meant in the church, what they meant in the Catechism, whose words are here appropriated, what they meant in the traditional theology of New-England, what they meant to Dr. Samuel Hopkins and to Dr. Samuel Spring, both of whom are explicit even to the rejection and condemnation of any denial of this established traditional meaning. I know of no evidence that at the time the Creed was written they had gained any new accepted interpretation. They require in the Creed therefore their ordinary sense.

Professor Stuart rejected this tenet, and apparently without any hesitation or misgiving. He defined his position in respect to the creed of Nicea by saying that "the thing aimed at was in substance to assert the idea of a distinction in the Godhead," which is perfectly true as the history shows. He said later that the fathers were "in substance right, their pneumatic philosophy plainly inadmissible."[1] He must have explained to himself his disagreement with the language of the Catechism in the Seminary Creed on the same principle. He held what the phrase "Eternal Son," in its traditional sense, stood for, viz., the doctrine of the Deity of Christ. But the traditional form of this belief, as embodied in this phrase, he denied. That is, he held to the substance of the doctrine, as this is an integral and essential part of the Creed, but he rejected a subsidiary, and as he regarded it, unessential and unbiblical form of that doctrine in its substance, though this is a part of the substance of the Creed.

This was done by him while he was in most intimate relations with the early Founders of the Seminary, particularly with the Associate Founder William Bartlet, who continued to pay bills for German books, which Professor Stuart imported almost by the cart-load, and who never was disturbed, I presume, because small men and narrow men cried out against his Professor's neology. Professor Stuart was called to account by Dr. Miller of Princeton, and in reply published a heterodox book and assiduously followed up all this "heterodoxy" by excursus after excursus in his commentaries, and by articles in the *Biblical Repository* and the *Bibliotheca Sacra*.

I have had myself a little experience in relation to this doctrine. I have been led to accept the ordinary church doctrine, and that of the Catechism and the Creed. I do not wish to

> "Compound for sins [I am] inclined to
> By damning those [I have] no mind to;"

but I am persuaded that Professor Stuart was wrong in the result of his exegesis on this point and in his interpretation of the history of the doctrine of the Eternal Sonship. I agree with the early Hopkinsians as well as with Charles Kingsley and Frederick D. Maurice in thinking this doctrine

---

[1] *Bibliotheca Sacra*, vii. p. 314.

an important one, and its rejection an error of some consequence. Coming early in my teaching at Andover to this conclusion, I have maintained the Creed on this point as I promised according to the best light God has given me. I soon learned, by the fire of questions poured in upon me that my pupils had been taught otherwise in another lecture room. I made no allusions to such teaching, but simply kept on with my own. It never occurred to me that somebody should be tried for "heterodoxy." If I had been a lawyer, certainly if I could have been a judge, I should have said that the article in the Creed was doubtless subscribed by my pupils' teacher in Christian theology, who had subscribed to the phrase "Eternal Son" in the Catechism as well as in the Creed, on the principle of "charitable construction," but being not a lawyer nor judge, but a Professor of Ecclesiastical History, I thought and still think that he subscribed on the principle which he now so vehemently repudiates, and which is expressed in the venerable New England formula, "for substance of doctrine."

This will I think make clear the full extent of my meaning. I reject all vague and loose applications of the phrase "for substance," but it has, I hold, its legitimate place in any requirement of subscription to the Seminary Creed which has even a decent regard to past usage, whether at Andover or in the church at large, or to the decisions of legal tribunals, or to the true intentions of such men as founded the Seminary whether Hopkinsians or Old Calvinists.

I know of but one important objection to this claim. It is said that the purpose of the Hopkinsians, who put the Creed into their Statutes, and came into the union on its acceptance by the Andover Founders, was to compel the Moderate Calvinists to greater strictness of belief at Andover than could be secured by a general consent to the Catechism; that in their opinion a general subscription or assent had let into the ministry a great many men who were doctrinally unsound, and that they intended to bar out such looseness. If now their own Creed is to be subscribed for substance, as the Catechism had been taken, the desired protection is thrown away, and the assumed purpose of the Founders is frustrated.

I think this is a fair criticism upon such interpretations and uses of the formula, "for substance of doctrine," as I have rejected and condemned.

But it goes no further. It overlooks important facts.

1. The fact that the Creed is a union Creed. What was its origin and first form is uncertain. One account represents that it was constructed for the Newbury Seminary, which was not intended to be a mere Hopkinsian affair, but broader. Another alleges that it was first presented to Dr. Spring by Dr. Pearson who represented the Andover Founders. All accounts agree that it was not intended for a mere party, and that it was finally accepted as a basis of union. It has from early times been called a "compromise" Creed. It certainly was designed to be comprehensive, and this is a more honorable description of it.

2. The fact that the Creed contains traditional phraseology which was accepted in its traditional meaning by some at least of those who entered into the union.

3. The fact that these men approved of this language being taken by other men with a new meaning, and that those who thus took it consented that such language should remain in the Creed.

One of these historical phrases is contained in the article: "[I believe] that Adam, the federal head and representative of the human race was placed in a state of probation and that in consequence of his disobedience all his descendants were constituted sinners." The phrase "federal head and representative" is the symbol of a distinct type of theology. In New England this had been, until the days of Jonathan Edwards, and particularly of Samuel Hopkins, the established system. It is the teaching of the Catechisms and the Confession. It was undergoing changes, but its essential idea that man's depravity comes to him not simply as an act of sovereignty but of law and justice was not yet abandoned. Emmons found it necessary to preach against it elaborately. Nor was it excluded from the Creed by the phrases "in consequence of" and " were constituted sinners." The latter is as old as the Vulgate.¹ It is Calvin's² language, and Turretin's.³ Professor Park comments on it as though it were distinctive of Emmons. He says: " In one and the same discourse the doctor [Emmons] calls Adam 'a federal head of the race' and criticises the Assembly's Catechism for teaching that Adam entered into a literal covenant with his Maker. So in one and the same sentence the Creed excludes all that the Catechism says in regard to the covenant of works, quotes the very language of Emmons, that all Adam's *descendants were constituted sinners*,' and also designates Adam as 'the federal head and representative of the race'. One sermon of Emmons is compressed into one article of the Creed." Unfortunately for this representation the sermon referred to was not preached until after the Creed was adopted, and the Seminary established; nor, so far as I can ascertain, was it published until 1860 in the edition of Emmons's works to which Dr. Park contributed a memoir. It is also well understood that Dr. Emmons was not entirely satisfied with the Creed. And, apart from all this, every old Calvinist could use the phrase " were constituted" and even " in consequence of," as well as the Hopkinsians. So that the article might with less forcing of its terms be harmonized with the Old Theology than with the New. Yet, on the other hand, it does not speak of the covenant of works, nor impute Adam's sin as guilt to his posterity, and the general shaping of the language in the context is all friendly to the new conceptions of moral agency which the Hopkinsians were zealously propagating. They too could live under this article in the Creed provided they could be allowed to accept the federal headship of Adam with a certain degree of latitude, in other words " for substance of doctrine." Professor Park really admits this to be the true explanation. For he adds to the words

¹ "Peccatores constituti sunt multi." Vulgate transl. of Rom. v. 19.

² " Quemadmodum enim per inobedientiam unius hominis peccatores constituti sunt multi: sic et per obedientiam unius justi constituentur multi." Com. on Rom. v. 19.

³ " Eadem quippe ratione constituimur peccatores in Adamo qua justi constituimur in Christo." *Inst. Theol. Elenct.*, Pars Prima, Locus Nonus *De Peccato*. Q. IX. § xvi. ed. Lugd. Batav. 1696, Vol. I. p. 681.

I have just quoted the statement, "The disclaimer of a word in a *literal* sense need not be a disclaimer of it in a *figurative* sense," and earlier on the same page, he says: "Those Hopkinsians, however, did not believe in any *literal* covenant of *works.* They could use the term figuratively, but would not insert the language of the Catechism into their Creed." *Their Creed!* It was not theirs alone. It was the Creed of the Federalists also, who could use the terms of this theology as the Hopkinsians could not. So that we are shut up to this conclusion. The Federalists put into, or found in, the Creed their favorite phrase "federal head and representative"; the Hopkinsians at least consented to its remaining there; and each party understood not only that it might bear a different meaning to the other, but that even if it did so, and the Creed were thus taken, it was satisfactorily taken, for it was accepted *for substance of doctrine.* Some criticism has been expended upon the Founders for their consenting to an ambiguous article. If the principle of the procedure were that each party should find his own doctrine by catching at one clause and ignoring another, by interpreting *federal headship* "figuratively" and *constituted* "literally," or *vice versa*, I think the procedure could not be defended. I suppose it to have been a larger, a firmly established and well understood principle on which they acted, namely, that whatever special theories these technical formulas suggested, and whatever preferences one person or another might entertain as respects these subsidiary forms of doctrine, the great fact was confessed of human depravity, so that men are acknowledged to be "morally incapable" of self-recovery, and to be in need of a Redeemer, and of regeneration by the Holy Spirit. Admit that the Article I have been considering can be accepted "for substance of doctrine," as I believe it has been subscribed from the first, and you simply apply to the Creed a well-known principle. Deny that this is legitimate, and you make an honest subscription impossible for any one but a Federal Calvinist, and discredit the entire history of the Seminary. It is discovered that Dr. Emmons once or twice, when he could not be misunderstood, used the older phraseology figuratively. And this is brought forward as a reason for giving the phrase the same interpretation in a carefully drawn Creed. In other words, because a preacher, in order to avoid a seemingly entire divorce of his thought from inherited principles, uses a familiar term in a way which suggests a connection between his own clearly explained and new views and the older theology, we have a right to understand such a phrase in a Creed to be *figurative*, and so are enabled to sign it literally, and avoid the offense of taking it substantially, as it has been taken from the time it was first written. I claim the right to abide by the accepted usage and the long established principle, and this not merely with reference to this article but wherever a similar exigency arises, always remembering the restrictions I have acknowledged.

There is one other general principle in the acceptance of theological creeds which was emphasized by Dr. Henry B. Smith, and which is of importance now. I remark therefore fourthly,

4. *I accept the Seminary Creed in its historical sense.*

I do not mean by this that opinions which it does not express may be read into it because they were entertained at the time it was written, and perhaps by the men who composed it; nor that opinions which they put into it may be taken out of it because, perchance, if they were living now, they would appoint a different creed.

The Associate Founders reserved to themselves the right for seven years to amend the Creed. They prohibited subsequent alterations. This does not define the nature of subscription, as some have affirmed; but it doubtless does exclude, indirectly or by necessary inference, any mutilation of the Creed in its administration, either by adding to it a tenet which it does not authorize, or subtracting from it one that it requires. To this extent it supplies a rule for subscription.

I agree to this rule, and do not assert anything contrary to it when I affirm the historical sense of the Creed. I intend by this formula to emphasize several things.

(1) The language of the Creed must be interpreted historically. Its traditional terms, not otherwise explained, must

have their traditional meaning. . Whatever of strictness, whatever of liberality, belongs to them when thus understood, enures to the subscriber now as at the first.

Such words and phrases are some already noticed: "only perfect rule of faith and practice," "three Persons," "same in substance," "equal in power and glory," "Adam, the federal head and representative," and so on.

Many Trinitarians hold to a personal or hypostatic subordination of the Son to the Father. So long as this is not understood to contradict what is affirmed by the phrase "same in substance," there is nothing in the Creed to exclude such a mode of belief. For the phrase "equality in power and glory" historically interpreted does not exclude either official or personal subordination, but only essential. One who denies the true Divinity of the Son could not sign the Creed honestly, but any believer in this doctrine, though a subordinationist, might accept it. We have here, as very often in the Creed, phrases which are not contracted but comprehensive, leaving room for many minor modifications of belief.

So the term "federal head," which also is left undefined, has a historical latitude of meaning. It came into vogue in opposition to an extreme type of Calvinism. It represented a new departure. It characterized a movement away from scholastic Calvinism in the direction of a Biblical Calvinism. It was a protest against an over-wrought doctrine of sovereignty, in the interest of human freedom. A man is not simply a creature, but a person, with whom God condescends to make a covenant. A distinguished theologian, to whom I have before referred, contends that the Creed must be taken in all its details, and cannot be taken as other Creeds are taken, but when he speaks of its federal terms he says, in language already partly quoted,[1] that the Founders "believed wisely in the 'covenant of redemption' and in the 'covenant of grace,' as these terms were understood by the divines whom they deemed most authoritative. Those Hopkinsians, however, did not believe in any *literal* covenant of *works*. They would use the term *figuratively* . . . " Thus by a

[1] *The Associate Creed of And. Theol. Sem.*, pp. 44, 45.

" wise" interpretation and a " figurative " interpretation, *all* the " details " of the Creed can be accepted literally!

But there is no need of such latitudinarian canons.

Taken historically all these terms are way-marks of progress along the line of modern theology, as it has more and more realized the true character of God as revealed in Christ, his overstepping the bounds of instituted law in the promises of his grace, his dealing with men as persons endowed by Him with inalienable rights. Professor Park has been wont to say that the covenant of works was made in Holland. It was — and it has in it the principle of liberty for which the Netherlanders fought by land and sea. I would not miss from the Creed Bullinger's " covenant of grace " or Cocceius's " covenant of works " in the form of Adam's federal headship. They are all there, and the signer of the Creed has his rights under them and to them. They are still a standing protest against an extreme type of Calvinism which after having been modified by Federalism suddenly shot up like Jonah's gourd in Emmonsism. The Creed, as Professor Park wisely but not figuratively claims, is " protective," if historically taken, and as a whole.

(2) Whenever traditional language is departed from and new phraseology introduced we are brought into special contact with the intention of the Founders.

In the legal interpretation of a document which is composed of printed matter and written statements, the latter have the preference in interpreting the author's purpose. It more especially expresses his mind and will.

This is an important principle in its application to the Seminary Creed.

There are three parts of the Creed in which these novelties of doctrine appear — the part which relates to original sin, the one which treats of redemption, and the part which treats of God's universal moral government; and the new matter introduced consists of either an enlargement or correction of the traditional theology in respect to two points, God's purpose of redemption, and the ethical principles by which He is governed in dealing with men ; these two aspects of truth being indeed but one principle by which Theology always makes what progress it achieves, namely, a more thoroughly ethical or Christian apprehension of God.

The truth of what I have been saying will appear to any one who examines intelligently a copy of the Creed, like the one I have prepared which shows by Italics those portions which are copied from the Shorter Catechism, by Roman type and black ink where the thoughts of the Westminster Standards are reproduced, and by red ink what is new.

"Every Professor on this foundation shall be a Master of Arts of the Protestant Reformed Religion, an ordained Minister of the Congregational or Presbyterian denomination, and shall sustain the character of a discreet, honest, learned, and devout Christian, an orthodox and consistent Calvinist; and, after a careful examination by the Visitors with reference to his religious principles, he shall, on the day of his inauguration, publicly make and subscribe a solemn declaration of his faith in Divine Revelation, and in the fundamental and distinguishing doctrines of the Gospel as expressed in the following Creed, which is supported by the infallible Revelation which God constantly makes of Himself in his works of creation, providence, and redemption, namely:—

"I believe that *there is* one, and *but one, . . . living and true God;* that *the word of God, . . . contained in the Scriptures of the Old and New Testament,*[1] *is the only* perfect rule of faith and practice; that agreeably to those Scriptures *God is a Spirit, infinite, eternal, and unchangeable in his being, wisdom, power, holiness, justice, goodness, and truth;* that *in the Godhead . . . are three Persons, the Father, the Son, and the Holy Ghost; and* that *these Three are One God, the same in substance, equal in power and glory;* that *God created man . . . after his own image, in knowledge, righteousness, and holiness;* that the glory of God *is man's chief end*, the enjoyment of God his supreme happiness; that this enjoyment is derived solely from conformity of heart to the moral character and will of God; that Adam, the federal head and

---

[1] S. C., Testaments.

representative of the human race, was placed in a state of probation, and that in consequence of his disobedience all his descendants were constituted sinners; that by nature every man is personally depraved, destitute of holiness, unlike and opposed to God; and that previously to the renewing agency of the Divine Spirit all his moral actions are adverse to the character and glory of God; that being morally incapable of recovering the image of his Creator, which was lost in **Adam,** every man is justly exposed to eternal damnation; so that, except a man be born again he cannot see the kingdom of God; that *God, . . . of his mere good pleasure, from all eternity, elected some to everlasting life,* and that he *entered into a covenant of grace to deliver them out of* this state *of sin and misery . . . by a Redeemer;* that *the only Redeemer of the elect is the eternal Son of God, who* for this purpose *became man, and . . .* continues *to be God and man in two distinct natures and one person forever;* that *Christ as our Redeemer executeth the office*[1] *of a Prophet, . . . Priest, and . . . King;* that agreeably to the covenant of redemption the Son of God, and he alone, by his suffering and death, has made atonement for the sins of all men; that *repentance, faith,* and holiness are the personal requisites in the Gospel scheme of salvation; that the *righteousness of Christ* is the *only* ground of a sinner's *justification;* that this righteousness is *received* through *faith,* and that this faith is **the gift of God;** so that our salvation is wholly of grace; that no means whatever can change the heart of a sinner and make it holy; that regeneration and sanctification are effects of the creating and renewing agency of the Holy Spirit, and that supreme love to God constitutes the essential difference between saints and sinners: that, by *convincing us of our sin and misery, enlightening our minds, . . . working faith in us, and renewing our wills,*[2] the *Holy Spirit* makes us *partakers of the* benefits of *redemption,* and that *the . . . ordinary means* by which these *benefits* are *communicated to us are the Word, sacraments, and prayer;* that *repentance* unto life, *faith to feed upon* Christ, *love* to God, *and new*

---

[1] *S. C.,* offices. [2] *S. C.,* will.

obedience are the appropriate qualifications for *the Lord's Supper,* and that a Christian Church ought to admit no person to its holy communion before he exhibit credible evidence of his godly sincerity; that perseverance in holiness is the only method of making our calling and election sure, and that the final perseverance of saints, though it is the effect of the special operation of God on their hearts, yet necessarily implies their own watchful diligence; that *they who are effectually called do in this life partake of justification, adoption,* and *sanctification and the several benefits which . . . do either accompany or flow from them;* that *the souls of believers are at their death made perfect in holiness, and do immediately pass into glory;* that *their bodies, being still united to Christ,* will *at the resurrection* be . . . *raised up to glory,* and that the saints will be *made perfectly blessed in the full enjoy*ment *of God to all eternity;* but that the wicked will awake to shame and everlasting contempt, and with devils be plunged into the lake that burneth with fire and brimstone for ever and ever. I moreover believe that God, *according to the counsel of his* own *will* and *for his own glory, hath foreordained whatsoever comes to pass,* and that all beings, actions, and events, both in the natural and moral world, are under his providential direction; that God's decrees perfectly consist with human liberty, God's universal agency with the agency of man, and man's dependence with his accountability; that man has understanding and corporeal strength to do all that God requires of him, so that nothing but the sinner's aversion to holiness prevents his salvation; that it is the prerogative of God to bring good out of evil, and that he will cause the wrath and rage of wicked men and devils to praise him; and that all the evil which has existed, and will forever exist, in the moral system, will eventually be made to promote a most important purpose under the wise and perfect administration of that Almighty Being who will cause all things to work for his own glory, and thus fulfil all his pleasure. And, furthermore, I do solemnly promise that I **will open and explain the Scriptures to my Pupils with integrity and faithfulness; that I will maintain and inculcate** the Christian faith as expressed in the Creed by me now repeated, together with all the other doctrines and duties of our holy Religion, so far as may appertain to my office, according to the best light God shall give me, and in opposition not only to atheists and infidels, but to Jews, Papists, Mahometans, Arians, Pelagians, Antinomians, Arminians, Socinians, Sabellians, Unitarians, and Universalists, and to all other heresies and errors, ancient or modern, which may be opposed to the Gospel of Christ or hazardous to the souls of men; that by my instruction, counsel, and example I will endeavor to promote true Piety and Godliness; that I will consult the good of this Institution and the peace of the Churches of our Lord Jesus Christ on all occasions; and that I will religiously conform to the Constitution and Laws of this Seminary, and to the Statutes of this Foundation."

. It follows from such a study of the Creed as I have indicated and from the application of the principle I have stated, that where contradiction would otherwise exist the controlling principle must be found in the interjected or new statement. The old cannot fetter the new; on the contrary the new may liberate the old.

Take the article about "federal head." If the Creed must be taken in its every detail, it asserts, as we have seen not figuratively but plainly and literally, the doctrine of the covenant of works. You cannot take this theory and at the same time accept one which contradicts it. But if any one should arise and take up the contention once so vigorously pressed against an Abbot Professor by Dr. Dana and Parsons Cooke and others, and insist that the Catechism and the Creed required that Professor to accept federal headship not in a figurative but in a literal sense, and that for nearly half a century he was guilty of a stupendous breach of trust and of violating his repeated solemn promises, a historical interpretation of the Creed will amply protect his good name. For if there is, as is claimed, a contradiction of theories in the Creed, the new formula has a superior power to the old, and so the Professor was quite in accord with the Creed in his lifelong rejection of federal headship and advocacy of the theory recognized if not with entire distinctness in the other portion of the article, at least in this when interpreted in the light of the prominence elsewhere given to the principle of personal moral agency.

Or take again the statement about a universal atonement. You cannot evidently harmonize universal atonement and limited atonement. Neither can you find in the Creed precisely the later theory of general atonement and particular redemption. The general atonement of the Creed is something wrought out under the "Covenant of Redemption." At the same time you cannot deny that under the phraseology of redemption is introduced a universal atonement; and this is not only unmistakably stated, but is the new element, and therefore *par excellence* to be insisted upon. All the previous language, therefore, which embodies the older theory of limited atonement must be qualified by this ruling article — in other words the whole doctrine of the covenant of grace, with particular election and redemption must be subsumed under the doctrine of universal redemption, and this again, so far as the covenant of redemption goes, must be adjusted to personal responsibility and the doctrine of retribution for the wicked at the day of final judgment.

Any one who takes the Creed in this way comes as near as it is possible to come to the mind of those who framed it. And it is no small honor to these men that at the early date when the Creed was written they were willing thus to modify the traditional Calvinism in the interest of a new movement of thought and to put two essential principles of the New Divinity — Universal Atonement and Personal Agency — into the Creed, and require all who taught in the Seminary to be faithful to them.

(3). There is room for a progressive interpretation and systemization of the truths of the Creed.

Dr. Park has enunciated the first and most important part of this proposition. He says, speaking of the Hopkinsian founders, "They were in favor of progress in the interpretation of the Creed, provided that the progress were toward the Hopkinsian interpretation of it." [1]

The Hopkinsian elements in the Creed have been already briefly characterized. They constitute the bulk of the additions to the Westminster statements. They include the principles of a universal atonement and personal agency.

But who will presume to say that these great principles had accomplished all their service for theology when they were put into the Creed, or at the close of any later period in the history of the Seminary? Who will doubt that the influence they already have exerted on the interpretation of other doctrines mentioned in the Creed must go on?

Historical interpretation gives us first the Creed in its meaning as understood by its framers: it also gives us the Creed as it proves to be a living fountain for others who receive it. No Creed is ever estimated aright or interpreted aright, until the principles in it which were vital to the authors of it are understood in their vitality, and vitality means always growth.

The other portion of my remark is no less true and important. The Creed admits of a progressive systematization of doctrine. I think it incites to such progress. It makes no attempt at systematic statement. It aims rather to enumerate the fundamental and distinguishing doctrines of the Gospel. Any work of systemizing is left to others. But its enumeration is the fruit of systemizing; and a historical interpretation, bringing to light its distinctive characteristics, shows how the inherited system is already modified, and how further changes are prophesied.

Put into the creed of old Calvinism, universal atonement, universal free moral agency, a higher conception of personality, and the system cannot remain what it was. The Hopkinsian founders were determined it should not, and the history of the Seminary proved they were right.

What a historical interpretation most emphatically suggests is the line along which this progress will move — what the direction of the systemizing process will be. It is from

[1] *The Associate Creed*, p. 94.

the formal to the real; from power to character, from work to person. So it has been in the entire history of theology as cultivated at Andover. Federalism gave way to the reality of a divine constitution, to laws of heredity and ethical responsibility. The work of Christ becomes more and more connected with his Person, the government of God with his character. The Creed opens the way to a more and more Christian conception of God and to a systemizing of all religious truth under this inspiration and with this centre. A Christocentric Theology — not a theology that centres in what is commonly understood by the words historic Christ, but one which centres in God as revealed in Christ — is just as admissible under the Creed at Andover as in any Church or School. For the Seminary Creed does not attempt to construct a completed system, nor to point out and prescribe in what the ultimate principle of the several truths it requires is to be found. The new elements are naturally thrown into special prominence, but they exclude nothing which is consistent with them. An experienced eye detects at once in this symbol the Creeds of Nicaea and Constantinople, the Creed of Chalcedon, the Augsburg Confession and the Westminster Standards, as well as the "improvements" of Edwards and Hopkins. And taking the whole into account it will be found to be a truer order and conception of its teaching to make the main historic root and stem of all Christian Theology its root and trunk rather than some one of its fruitful branches. Calvin had a true instinct when he arranged the topics of Christian faith, in the first edition of his *Institutes*, according to the scheme of the *Apostles' Creed*.

4. The truths of the Seminary Creed may be adjusted to a larger knowledge and life than were open to its framers. A historical study and interpretation of the Creed shows that these truths came to these men as living and fruitful principles, and it is of the very nature of such truths to find new application and service in new forms.

It is one of the constant surprises to a student of the intellectual and moral history of man to find how differently a system, which has been superseded, appears when it is approached from the other side and followed through its period of conflict to the time when it wins its victory, and for this reason passes more and more out of sight. Its moving principles are not thus lost, rather they are now appropriated and assimilated and become a part of the life and working power of the Church. What if a man sees a larger truth in election than individual salvation, is he denying his Calvinistic creed? What if he discern, that the principle of probation, on the basis of atonement, when once admitted, will not cramp itself to the meagre knowledge men had a hundred years ago of the perishing millions of Africa and Asia? Does he abandon this principle because he trusts it? What if Christianity seems to him more and more to be the key to history, more and more evidently to mean the powers of recovery which God is pouring into the growing life of the ages, and so with a simpler faith than ever before he turns to the Cross and the Incarnation as the master light of all his seeing, does he thereby renounce his connection with men who could not stop when they had written the article upon the doom of the wicked, but added a new close to their Creed in this stately and comprehensive confession: "(I believe) that it is the prerogative of God to bring good out of evil, and that he will cause the wrath and rage of wicked men to praise Him ; and that all the evil which has existed, and which will forever exist in the moral system will eventually be made to promote a most important purpose under the wise and perfect administration of that Almighty Being who will cause all things to work for His own glory, and thus fulfil all His pleasure"?

When the controversy began, whose outcome is the present trial, an editorial in the *Congregationalist* described the Seminary Creed, with the Visitorial system, "as a complicated and iron-bound endeavor to anchor the orthodoxy of the future as by chain cable to one of its particular phases in the past." The issue thus made in the beginning is the real question at the end. It is a testing question for you, Mr. President and Gentlemen, as well as for me. You are on trial no less than I. The Seminary is on trial. Is it committed to the maintenance of transient opinion, or is there a truer interpretation of its Creed? Is your office like that of a tither of mint, anise and cummin, or are you interpreters of a religious Creed whose words are to be understood in their connections with the life of the Church and with Him whose teaching is Spirit and life?

I plead for no license of interpretation, for no violation of any just law of interpretation, for no departure from the natural, grammatical, historic meaning of terms and phrases — but I ask for breadth, insight and justice. I do not ask you to make the Creed utter what we might suppose its framers would say were they living now, but did not because they flourished nearly a century ago — *ita Lex scripta est*. This is the rule. But finding out what it says, I ask you to interpret it as a whole, to admit the impossibility of making every article in its obligation complete in itself, or any phrase literally binding which is traditional and contradictory to what is new in the Creed and therefore controlling, and I especially ask your attention to the facts that at the beginning of my acceptance of the Creed I am reminded of God's constant revelation of Himself, and near its close I make this solemn promise, that I will teach the Christian faith as expressed in the Creed . . together with the other doctrines and duties of our holy religion, so far as may appertain to my office, ACCORDING TO THE BEST LIGHT GOD SHALL GIVE ME. I have tried to follow this light. Until these recent unhappy disputes I have never heard it questioned at Andover but that the Creed could be taken on the principles I have stated. I came with the understanding that it was thus liberally interpreted and administered. I supposed such a policy to be as much a recognized part of the institution as having a library or daily prayers. I believe that it alone really fulfils the true intention of the Founders. Among my reasons for such a faith are these:

1. The Seminary was organized and its Creed drawn to be a means of union of the various parties, or as they were called, denominations, of Orthodox Congregationalists then existing. Few realize how many and deep were the divisions in those

days — leaving out of account the great schism which was hastening — how they fomented jealousies and suspicions and separated brethren into cliques and factions and arrayed them as supporters of this periodical or that, and even of different missionary organizations. The necessity of union was paramount in the minds of the leading men who founded the Seminary. It appears abundantly in their published correspondence, and will not I presume be disputed. Dr. Bacon at the Semi-Centennial of the Seminary expressed the common and undisputed opinion when he characterized the establishment of the Seminary as "an epoch in the history of New England theology," and added "It was founded, not for the special interest of any one locality or district, nor for the special system of any theological discoverer, but for the common interest of the churches, and for the common orthodoxy of Massachusetts and New England. It was pledged at the outset to a large and tolerant orthodoxy, as distinguished from the intolerance and contentiousness by which the little cliques and parties that arise in a particular locality and around a particular great man are too often characterized."[1] Unless there can be room in its Faculty for men who are loyal to what Dr. Bacon calls "the common orthodoxy of Massachusetts and New England" (by which he does not mean the ordinary opinion, or that of a majority), but who differ from others of their brethren as Dr. Stiles differed from Dr. Hopkins, or Emmons from Burton, or French from Spring, all of whom Dr. Bacon regards as within the purpose of the Creed,[2] the Seminary fails to fulfil the object for which it was founded.

2. The general structure of the Creed and the clauses respecting God's constant revelation and the promise which implies new light, favor the same conclusion.

3. The Constitution of the Seminary implies throughout the faith of the Founders in the advancement of religious knowledge. It bears throughout the impress of the broad and

---

[1] Memorial of the Fiftieth Anniversary, Andover: Published by Warren F. Draper, 1859, p. 101. See also *The Panoplist* IV. pp. 372, 373.

[2] *Memorial*, p. 90.

liberal mind of Dr. Pearson, as well as of the generosity and public spirit of the donors. It was founded to increase "the number of *learned* and *able* Defenders of the Gospel of Christ as well as of orthodox, pious, and zealous Ministers of the New Testament." A three years' residence was deemed "a period scarcely sufficient for acquiring that fund of knowledge which is necessary for a Minister of the Gospel." Greek and Hebrew were made obligatory through the course. Provision was made by which new foundations, whether chairs of instruction or scholarships, should be increased. The curriculum sketched at the outset is larger than has yet been realized. A theological university, exceeding any thing before known, was in mind. There was threatening what was regarded as a great religious defection. It was to be met not simply with religious zeal and asserted authority of revelation, but with all available weapons of reason and learning. A perusal of Mr. Abbot's will by which the Seminary received a most munificent bequest will satisfy any reader of the generous purposes of knowledge with which the institution was started. But is it possible to suppose that all this was done in the expectation that there would be no advancement in the understanding of truth, or that men would not be allowed, while holding fast to the principles of the Creed, to put them in new relations and gain new results?

What actually was done is well known in the case of Professor Stuart. His friends were at times anxious lest he was verging to Sabellianism or rationalism, and he was always under fire, but Mr. Bartlet went on with his remittances, and when once a Committee of the Trustees remonstrated at certain offences committed in the first edition of his commentary on Romans, Professor Stuart replied that he considered the interference "inquisitorial," and this ended the matter. He taught in variance from the Creed all his life on "The Eternal Sonship," and if, as I suppose to be true, his opinion is now generally rejected, this also shows the wisdom of trusting to the power of truth in such matters.

The character of the advisers of the Associate Founders, their humility, and their faith in doctrinal progress, the school of theology to which they belonged, concur to the same result. I have spoken thus far of the so-called Original Founders particularly, but not exclusively, for the Associate Foundation became a part of one and the same institution.

I turn now to the Hopkinsians. They had the spirit of their great leader whose words I will quote from the memoir by Dr. Park.

" When tired," says his biographer, " of hearing the stale charge that he had started new doctrines into life, he responds : ' I now declare, I had much rather publish *New Divinity* than any other. And the more of this the better, — if it be but true. Nor do I think any doctrine can be " too strange to be true." I should think it hardly worth while to write, if I had nothing *new* to say.' In his ' Animadversions on Mr. Hart's Late Dialogue,' Hopkins alludes to his having been falsely accused of propounding new theories, and replies : ' This he [Mr. Hart] has done over and over again, about a dozen times. He calls them " new doctrines," " a new system or rather chaos of divinity," " upstart errors," etc. And the teachers of them he calls " new apostles," " new divines," " new teachers," etc. — If this were true, I see not what reason there would be to make such a great outcry about it. There is really no evidence against these doctrines. It is at least *possible*, that there is some truth contained in the Bible, which has not been commonly taught; yea, has never been mentioned by any writer since the apostles; and whenever that shall be discovered and brought out, it will be *new*. And who knows but that some such *new* discoveries may be made in our day? If so, unhappy and very guilty will be the man who shall attempt to fright people, and raise their prejudices against it, by raising the cry of New Divinity. Indeed, I question whether an author can, with a right temper and view, take this method to run any doctrine down, by appealing to the prejudices of people, and keeping up a constant loud cry of *new*, *upstart* divinity.' " [1]

" ' There is no reason to doubt,' he says in his seventy-second year, ' that light will so increase in the church, and men will be raised up, who will make such advances in opening the Scripture and in the knowledge of divine truth, that what is now done and

---

[1] Works of Samuel Hopkins, D.D. Boston, Doctrinal Tract and Book Society, 1852. Vol. I., pp. 177, 178.

written will be so far superseded as to appear imperfect and inconsiderable, compared with that superior light, with which the church will then be blessed.'"[1]

It should go without saying that if a Professor, following the best light which dawns upon him, finds himself wandering away from the Creed he is not to set up his private judgment and conceal his divergence, nor if the variation puts him in contradiction to the essential principles and the intent of the Creed do I raise any question as to his duty or yours.

What I maintain, and where I abide in good conscience is this: I have not thus violated my obligations under the Creed, even upon a close and technical construction of them. And if, as I also maintain, the Creed is a summary of principles which are to be applied and developed from generation to generation, I have done something far better and more faithful than a literal repetition of them — I have used them, and with them have confronted present great and important questions of religious thought and life.

What is proposed to be done? To remove, directly or indirectly almost, perhaps quite, an entire Faculty, and to proclaim to the world that an institution started as was Andover Seminary has outlived its usefulness. Not that men cannot be found to fill its chairs who may think that they are taking the Creed literally when they confess at once a limited atonement and an unlimited one, a federal headship which is figurative and an eternal Sonship which is temporal. Not that others still, if necessary, cannot be discovered who hold that when Paul says, "as many as have sinned without law shall also perish without law," he cuts off all hope for every heathen, and no offence need be taken at reading the word all into the Creed when it says that the effectually called receive the blessings of salvation in this life, or who still adhere to the theology of the covenants — but it will indeed be a new Andover when such principles of interpretation of the Creed are sanctioned. And how long can such a method of administration be perpetuated? If indeed the language of the instrument were perfectly plain,

[1] *Ibid.*, p. 231.

the argument from consequences would be irrelevant here. But instead of a perspicuous utterance there is at most silence, while for a liberal interpretation are the deep suggestions of its great doctrines of atonement and moral agency, of the Incarnation and an infinitely wise and benevolent and sovereign God, with his purpose binding together the ages, and the declaration of God's larger and constant revelation in his works, and the solemn promise exacted to look for light, and the happy auguries and peaceful promise and generous surroundings of its birth, and the expectation of the Founders that they had established an institution which should continue to bless the world so long as the sun and moon shall endure.

I am conscious of no desire paramount to the good of the Seminary. The finger of scorn is pointed at what is claimed to be the small support gained for the opinions expressed in Progressive Orthodoxy. We do not set up those opinions as a standard for Andover Professors. Some of our colleagues, esteemed and beloved, may not hold them. I really do not know where they all stand. And, besides, it *is* a new thing for men who demand fidelity to the Hopkinsian Founders to make the degree of present acceptance of a tenet the test of its truth! Writing in his seventy-fifth year Dr. Samuel Hopkins said,

"About forty years ago there were but few, perhaps not more than four or five, who espoused the sentiments which since have been called *Edwardean* and *New Divinity*, and, since after some improvement was made upon them, *Hopkintonian* or *Hopkinsian* sentiments. But those sentiments have so spread since that time among ministers, especially those who have since come on the stage, that there are now more than one hundred in the ministry, who espouse the same sentiments, in the United States of America. And the number appears to be fast increasing, and these sentiments appear to be coming more and more into credit, and are to be understood, and the odium which has been cast on them, and those who preached them, is greatly subdued." [1]

[1] Hopkins's Works, I., 237, 238.

His biographer adds that "the spirit of the new Divinity was in the hearts of thousands, who did not favor it in all its forms. The term ' Hopkinsian ' soon became the common designation of those evangelical or orthodox divines who favored the doctrines of general atonement, natural ability, the active nature of all holiness and sin, and the Justice of God in imputing to men none but their own personal transgressions."[1] That is, in 1756 there were five clergymen who dared believe that men are not punished for a sin they did not commit, and that Christ died for all men, and now I suppose there are not so many in New England who would be willing to be known as holding the opposite. Universal atonement is the orthodox belief.

It is idle to question that in all lands, in all evangelical churches to-day the question of the personal relation of Christ to the entire race for which He died is receiving an attention never before given to it. The Church at large has never yet passed upon it. It was not before the minds of the authors of the Catechism or of the Seminary Creed. It could not be. Providence shapes problems for the Church. It puts this one before us. It would be at least doubtful whether if the Creed contained some expressions which might be used to exclude the new doctrine it would not be an unwarrantable use of an incidental phrase to make it interdictive and decisive of a question out of the purview of the framers. Fortunately there is no such difficulty to be settled. The Creed admits by its silence and by its principles, at least as a legitimate inquiry, all that has been contended for by me in the *Review* and in *Progressive Orthodoxy.*

I offer this as a complete and full justification against the charges of the complainants.

[1] *Ibid.*, p. 238.

NOTE.

The following are the particular charges which are specially considered, or referred to, in the foregoing argument: —

Page 9.

"1. That the Bible is not 'the only perfect rule of faith and practice,' but is fallible and untrustworthy even in some of its religious teachings."

Page 20.

"2. That Christ in the days of his humiliation was a finite being, limited in all his attributes, capacities and attainments; in other words, was not 'God and Man.'"

Page 20.

"3. That no man has power or capacity to repent without knowledge of God in Christ."

Page 24.

"4. That mankind, save as they have received a knowledge of 'the historic Christ,' are not sinners, or, if they are, not of such sinfulness as to be in danger of being lost. ('*Progressive Orthodoxy*,' p. 55.)"

Page 25.

"5. That no man can be lost without having had knowledge of Christ. ('*Progressive Orthodoxy*,' pp. 63, 64.)"

Page 25.

"6. That the atonement of Christ consists essentially and chiefly in his becoming identified with the human race through his incarnation, in order that, by his union with men, he might endow them with the power to repent, and thus impart to them an augmented value in the view of God, and so render God propitious towards them."

Page 26.

"7. That the Trinity is modal, or monarchian, and not a Trinity of Persons."

Page 31.

"8. That the work of the Holy Spirit is chiefly confined to the sphere of historic Christianity."

Page 31.

"9. That without the knowledge of God in Christ, men do not deserve the punishment of the law, and that therefore their salvation is not 'wholly of grace.'"

Page 31.

"10. That faith ought to be scientific and rational rather than scriptural."

Page 33.

"11. That there is, and will be, probation after death for all men who do not decisively reject Christ during the earthly life; and that this should be emphasized, made influential, and even central in systematic theology."

The "Reply" to which reference is made on page 24 and elsewhere, is the answer filed by the respondent with the Board of Visitors on Nov. 30, 1886, and extensively published by the daily press.

STATEMENT OF PROFESSOR WILLIAM J. TUCKER.

Mr. President, and Gentlemen of the Board of Visitors:

It is not my intention, nor the intention of the respondents who may follow me, to traverse the ground covered in the argument of our honored colleague. We adopt by common consent the views therein expressed in regard to the Creed of the Seminary, and the terms of subscription to it, and we accept the answer therein made to the charges and specifications of the complainants. If now we make further demands upon your time in this hearing — and our demands will not be large — to meet the charges as preferred against us in person, it is because of personal relations which we severally hold to the Creed of the Seminary. There are obligations which apply to us in common, and there are obligations and requirements which derive a special meaning and force from their application to the departments which we individually represent.

Before I pass to my personal defense, I ask your indulgence for the moment to an incidental matter of general interest. During the progress of this hearing, frequent reference has been made in somewhat depreciatory language to the interposition of counsel on behalf of the respondents. I call up the fact of the employment of counsel not for apology but for explanation. The first intimation which we received of these proceedings was in the receipt of a communication from your honorable body containing the charges and specifications of the complainants, accompanied by an order that we file an answer within fifteen days. We had no knowledge whatever of the affair beyond that which was conveyed in the communication before us. We knew nothing of the origin or motive or resources of the prosecution. It seemed to be an organized movement and representative of something, for one of the prosecutors signed himself "a trustee" and the others "a committee of certain of the Alumni."

To this communication we made reply at the specified time, not only without counsel, but without having taken legal advice; and each man made reply for himself, not as in the answer to the amended complaint, when we united in a common reply. It was not until the case began to assume a judicial character under the subsequent orders of your Board, that we introduced counsel, and from that time the case has gone on upon its legal or theological side as either issue has for the time been uppermost. I have recalled this fact, in reference to our first answer, to your knowledge, because it has been overlooked and obscured. You will bear us witness that the original reply anticipated all legal procedures, and that it was direct, frank and specific upon the theological questions at issue.

The charge, Mr. President, upon which I appear before you in this hearing, I now understand to be that of heterodoxy in respect to the Creed, involving the more special charge upon myself in connection with Professor Smyth, according to the terms of our foundations, that I am "not an orthodox and consistent Calvinist." Up to the closing argument for the complainants, there seemed to be no little confusion between the complainants and their counsel as to the exact nature of this prosecution, whether it were for breach of trust or for heresy. The argument to which I have referred seems to settle this question. The Counsel said; "There is no breach of trust suggested against Professor Smyth by me, and there has not been. It must have been only casually, by inference, if it has ever been introduced into these proceedings. We never expected any such thing would be done." And again "I should suppose that if any doctrine, held as a distinctive doctrine by this interesting company of persons, not intended in any way to be approved, commended or forwarded by the Foundation of the Andover Theological Seminary, who seemed to be grouped here at the end of the creed, almost on the principle of the tares, binding them in bundles to burn them, — ' In opposition not only to Atheists and Infidels, but to Jews, Papists, Mahometans, Arians, Pelagians, Antinominians, Arminians, Socinians, Sabellians, Unitarians, and Universalists, and all other heresies and errors,' — I should suppose that there could be no doubt that if there were anything which could be included in that list, could be proved and established in this theological discussion as having been taught by a professor at Andover, you would have no difficulty about it."

Assuming from these admissions that the charge is that of heterodoxy in regard to the Creed of the Seminary, I will say that I accept without question, whatever of responsibility may attach to the publication of the articles, and of the book, from which the citations in support of the charges have been drawn. I make no distinction between what I teach and what I publish, alone or in responsible connection with others, save in this regard — and upon this distinction I do insist — I endeavor to teach according to the natural proportion of truth; I publish according to the exigencies of public discussion, claiming in this regard the unvexed right of publication, subject only to fidelity to the Constitution and Creed of the Seminary in the subject-matter of what I publish.

My defense is twofold. It covers my personal and my official relation to the Creed.

I answer first; that the theology of "Progressive Orthodoxy" is a natural and legitimate outcome of the Creed of the Seminary, especially at the point of greatest contention, that of probation for all men under the gospel. I may be allowed to say that there is a presumption in favor of this theology as consistent with the teachings of Andover, because it is held and put forth by men who are theologically the product of Andover or of the influences which made Andover.

In the original form under which the charges were preferred, three of the four complainants signed themselves as a Committee of "certain of the Alumni." This term alumni has in itself a significance which does not necessarily attach to any merely official connection with the Seminary. It is suggestive of the more sensitive, if less responsible, relations of loyalty and affection. In this respect to be an alumnus is more than to be a professor or a trustee or a visitor. When therefore a case is made up of certain alumni against certain professors, it seems to be a case in the interest of loyalty.

But, in the present instance, of the five accused professors four are alumni, and of the one who is not an alumnus, though for a considerable time a graduate student, it may fairly be said that in what belongs to him by inheritance, and in what he has earned by long and devoted service, he represents more, than any other one of us, of this quality of affectionate loyalty. Another professor, I refer to Professor Churchill, passed immediately upon graduation into the service of the Seminary. And of the remaining three, Professors Harris, Hincks and myself, graduating within two or three years of one another, we came back into the service of the Seminary chiefly because we were alumni. We were not ambitious of the positions which we now fill. Content and satisfied in the work of the pastorate we returned to Andover at its call because we loved Andover. We had its traditions; our roots were in its soil. And coming to our chairs from the pastorate, not from fields of speculative thought, but from contact with men, we brought with us those conceptions of Christian truth which we have since tried to unfold. For myself it is absolutely true, that I am conscious of holding no other gospel to-day, in any other spirit or with any other conclusion, than that which I held in my active ministry, and it never occurred to me, though in the course of my ministry I crossed and recrossed the line of my denomination that Andover would ever summon me to account for my holding of the gospel as contrary to her traditions, her teachings and her spirit. I speak now as an alumnus, not as a professor. And in so speaking I think that I represent at least "certain of the Alumni." For I remember that when attempts have been made at regularly constituted alumni meetings to inaugurate proceedings like the present, they have ignominiously failed.

I am singled out, Mr. President, in connection with Professor Smyth upon the charge, related, I suppose to the theory of a Christian probation, that I am not an "orthodox and consistent Calvinist." You will allow me to say, without argument, that if I am not "an orthodox and consistent Calvinist," according to the Creed, in my theological convictions and methods, I am nothing. Without permitting myself to put that which is of a name or of a school above that which is of Christ, I believe in Calvinism, not as the Creed found it but as the Creed tried to leave it. I believe in its ruling idea and method as against the idea and method to which it is historically opposed. I locate the hope of man in the power and purpose of God, not in exaggerated and unreal notions of man's ability. Christianity is to me above all things a religion of motives. Calvinism is a religion of motives. It emphasizes the "power of God" unto salvation, though in its older and higher forms it limits the application of the power, shutting it up within an arbitrary election. The Creed takes up this idea of power which inheres in Calvinism and gives it breadth and freedom. To me it is an inspiration, remembering the struggle of which the Creed bears ineradicable marks, which makes the Creed a thing of life and not an instrument of bondage — to me it is an inspiration to follow this idea of divine power and purpose, which the Creed inherits from the Catechism, as it feels its way along till it finds the gateway of universal Atonement, through which it pours its now free and invigorating current. The current which runs through the Creed is Calvinism. The Creed widens its banks. And the natural culmination of the Calvinism of the Creed lies to my mind in the very hope of which I am chiefly called in question, the hope which I reverently entertain without equivocation and without excuse, that God according to the eternal purpose which he purposed in Christ, will see to it that every soul comes into some real relation to Christ's atoning sacrifice before any soul passes into the eternal condemnation. And in the name of the Calvinism of the Creed I protest against the contention of those who, reaching in some other way a like conclusion, who are indignant if a theology with a narrower conclusion is imputed to them, do yet charge me with being heterodox toward the Creed, if I believe that God is saving such as are being saved in the way of consistent Calvinism and of orthodox Christianity.

I have used the latter term, orthodox Christianity, advisedly. For as I believe the philosophy of those who deny the possibility of a Christian probation to all men, leads away from orthodox Christianity. If there be any in these days who accept the dogma of the universal perdition of the race outside Christianity, these are removed from any interest or concern in existing controversies. But among those who refuse to accept the dogma, there can be but two parties, those who look upon man as the subject of redemption, and therefore accessible in some way and at some time to the motives of redemption, and those who look upon man as having a sufficiency of motive in himself under the light of nature, and under the work of the Spirit independent of the cross of Christ. Can there be any doubt as to which of these theories is the more closely related to Calvinism and which to Unitarianism? Can there be any doubt toward which the Creed of the Seminary inclines? If Andover Seminary was established to oppose and counteract any influence it was that of Unitarianism. For this object the more extreme parties in orthodoxy were willing to sink their differences and unite. This is an historic fact which none will dispute. Now I do not charge upon those who hold the theory of salvation under the light of nature that they are Unitarians, but I do wish to suggest to you that in their eagerness to use any and all arguments to combat the theory of a Christian probation, they are making themselves exceedingly familiar with the old time arguments of Unitarians in regard to Christian Missions. And I wish to suggest further that in the impending conflict in this country between Chris-

tianity and Naturalism it is of some consequence which way
the influence of Andover counts. The present controversy
may seem provincial. It is called so by some who have not
discovered its larger bearings. But it is the door through
which New England theology is to enter in and take its part
in the contention to which I have referred, the contention
between Christianity and Naturalism. And my study of the
Creed convinces me that Andover has in hand a weapon of
exceeding keenness and power if its edge is not turned in
the very opening of the conflict.

My second answer has to do with my official relation to
the Creed. I am a teacher of Homiletics. It is my duty to
instruct in regard to the subject-matter and the method of
preaching, and show how the truth can be made the instrument of conviction and persuasion in bringing men to
Christ.

I answer then in the second place that the method of the
theology which is called in question best satisfies the requirements of the Creed in respect to the conduct of my professorship. I am called upon in that Creed to teach the truth
in opposition to all errors which are "hazardous to the souls
of men." To me this is the most serious part of the Creed.
Even in the enumeration of errors which gives to the Creed
a somewhat belligerent tone one detects the earnestness and
scope of its intention. It was this part of the Creed which
chiefly arrested my attention when examining it with a view
to subscription. And the terms of my subscription, accord
ing to the testimony which I have given you, were in these
words — " The Creed which I am about to read, and to which
I shall subscribe, I fully accept as setting forth the truth
against the errors which it was designed to meet." How
was I to carry out the terms of my subscription? How was
I to fulfil the intention of the Creed? The question was
one of method. I tried to answer it according to my experience. I came to my professorship after a pastoral service of
twelve years. The two communities in which my pastorates
were served gave me ready and full access to the thoughts
of men, especially to the thoughts of men in their scepticism

and oppositions to Christianity. And under the study which this intercourse gave me I discovered that error has two means of livelihood. A given error lives because of the truth in it. No error is all error. And it lives because of the error in the truth which opposes it. Error thrives upon all insincerities and exaggerations in the holding of truth. Mohammedanism, to take a remote example of the errors which I am to oppose, lives upon the truth which inheres in it, the truth of God in His unity and sovereignty: a truth so profound and vital that it is impossible for any but the purest type of Christianity to live beside it: a truth which makes it, in the presence of an impure Christianity, a perpetual "scourge of God." Take now an error specified in the Creed which is close at hand and most involved in the present controversy, that of Universalism. Upon what does Universalism rely for its increase? Not simply upon the truths which it holds, for most of these are held in common with the Evangelical denominations. Universalism thrives upon the errors of orthodoxy, upon all exaggerated, untenable, insincere assertions of the orthodox faith. My complainants charge "Progressive Orthodoxy" with teaching toward Universalism. What is their alternative under the Creed? The interpretation which they have sought to put upon the Creed to counteract this tendency is to be seen in their use of the clause respecting those who are effectually called as *in this life* partaking of justification, adoption and sanctification. What must this clause say to be of use to them? Why this, that those only who do *in this life* share in the results of effectual calling, justification, adoption, sanctification and the like, are effectually called, that is saved: all others, including the mass of the heathen, and, by logic, all infants are lost. Now if this is the true interpretation of the Creed it is to be taught. I am to teach my pupils to preach it. Suppose they do preach it; what better means can they take to build up Universalism? Is this the way to meet that error? What is the intellectual difficulty which Universalism seeks to meet and solve? I have not found many men who disbelieved in future punishment. I have not found it difficult to gain a response from any congregation when preaching upon this doctrine. The intellectual difficulty does not lie in the doctrine itself, fearful as it is, but in the injustice and inequalities of application which attach to it under some representations of it. The state of the public mind in respect to this doctrine of future punishment, so far as I have observed, is precisely like that which existed fifty years ago in respect to the doctrine of election. Men were not then in revolt against the sovereignty of God. They were in revolt against the narrow and arbitrary application of it. They are in revolt to-day against a like narrow and arbitrary application of the Divine justice; they are in revolt against the assertion of a dogma, which assigns the greater part of the human race to perdition without the opportunity of accepting or rejecting its Redeemer.

This much for the Creed on its apologetic side as related to the pulpit. I am more concerned with the Creed on its evangelistic side, for the great end which it has in view is the conversion of men under the proclamation of the gospel. But here it is charged that "Progressive Orthodoxy" takes away the urgency of the gospel, that it changes the accent of the gospel, in the emphasis which it naturally lays on the present. To which I reply that the view there set forth ought to produce, and does produce when accepted, precisely the opposite effect. Why is the preacher able to say to men, "Now is the accepted time." "Now is the day of salvation"? Is it not because of the offer of salvation which has gone before? Suppose a missionary to go up and down Africa and without first offering Christ to men to say to them "Now is the accepted time!" what meaning would his words convey? Words take their meaning from their connection. It is the incoming of Christianity, the offer of salvation, which puts such a meaning into the "now" of men's lives. So the Baptist as he saw the Jewish skies beginning to flush under the dawn of Christianity cried out with a new meaning, "Repent, the kingdom of heaven is at hand." So Peter at Pentecost, standing in the shadow of the cross, and beside the open grave of Christ, could say to men with such result as followed, "Repent and be baptized every one of you for the remission of sins." And so Paul at Athens, proclaiming a risen Christ could declare that the times of ignorance God had overlooked, but now he commandeth all men everywhere to repent. We are so familiar with the call to repentance that we forget that it assumes the gospel. Herein lay the irrelevancy of all the passages quoted by Dr. Dexter from the sermons of the early New England divines to prove their opinion upon the question of a future probation. They all assumed that their hearers had now the full opportunity of accepting Christ and therefore there would be no other and better one, an inference with which we are in full agreement. Herein too lay the significance of the sermon introduced by Dr. Wellman into his argument, in which he tried to show how those who believed in the possibilities of men in Christ because of their vital relation to him even in their sin, would preach to sinners. Listening to that sermon, even under its unsympathetic statement of the idea, I forgot for the time the argument, I became indifferent to the irony, I felt the truth. So I try to teach men to preach Christ to their fellow-men so that they can say to them, *now*, and now only, is the accepted time; for now, you have your possibilities in Christ; now your decision is full and final.

Now am I right or am I wrong in this conception of the Creed as related to preaching? I ask your opinion. I want to know in some authoritative way whether or no this is heterodoxy. I ask for no charitable construction of the Creed in any other than the legal sense of the term. I want to know what its working construction is. I want to know how I am to handle the creed in my endeavor to train men to preach the truth, whether they are dealing with error, or whether they are dealing with the glorious imperatives of the gospel.

I conclude this personal statement with a brief reference to the changes which have taken place since my official connection with the Seminary. I came to Andover in 1880. That was two years before the present disturbance. My term of service covers the transition from what is called the old to what is called the new. The term new departure is not our term. Two years before the election of Dr. Newman Smyth to the chair of Theology, that is in the year 1880, the class entering the Seminary numbered ten. The year following, 1881, the entering class numbered five. If charges are brought against the present administration of Andover, tending to show its decline, let care be taken in the matter of dates. To-day there are forty-eight undergraduate students at Andover, — this does not include fourth year men or fellows — giving the Seminary the second place in numbers among the four Congregational Seminaries of New England and if I am not mistaken the second place among the Congregational Seminaries in the country in the number of regular students. And during these years of suspicion and opposition the graduates of the Seminary have passed without exception into the service of the churches. They all fill honored pastorates in New England and throughout the country. Meanwhile I know of no function of the Seminary which has been reduced. I know of no relation to the churches which has been broken, not even that relation which allows the return to the Seminary of gifts of money. During the past year not less than eighty thousand dollars have been added intelligently to the funds of the Seminary. Andover is furnishing to-day as always men for the established pastorates, for arduous and difficult service on the frontier; she has her quota of men knocking and in waiting at the doors of the American Board. So far as I can discover as an alumnus the Andover that is, is in spirit and in method and in result the Andover that was. The true continuity, the real succession is there, and there along the line of present development, I most assuredly believe that the true continuity, the real succession will give, under any and all possible contingencies, the Andover of the future. If I did not believe this in the loyalty of my heart as an alumnus of the Seminary, I should not for a moment remain in its official service. Indeed Mr. President I may say without affectation that as this hearing has proceeded my chief interest and concern has changed. I came here anxious to vindicate my rights in my present holding of truth under the Creed of the Seminary. It is for you to judge whether the vindication has been made. But my greater anxiety in your decision is for the Seminary itself. A right is a right in respect to any man and his work. But what are the interests of five men as compared with the interests of an institution. I agree with the position of the complainants which subordinates our personal and professorial interests to those which are higher. I have asked for no charitable construction of the Creed in behalf of our teachings. I ask for no kind of charity in dealing with our personal interests.

But for the Seminary my thought is more urgent. Underneath any rights which inhere in my professorship, I am conscious of the assertion of the deeper and inalienable rights which belong to me as an alumnus of Andover, and as such I venture to ask in my anxiety — what is to be its future? I ask it in the name of its past. Who has the right to affirm of the past of any time that it is conservative and not progressive? Who has the right to say this of Andover in the light of its history? The men who founded Andover builded well, consciously well, but they builded even better than they knew, and I believe that they to-day rejoice that they builded better than they knew — that the principles which they forced into the Creed were wider and more far reaching than they dared to conceive.

I ask in the name of a great number of living and working alumni, many of whom are in intellectual sympathy with its current theology, and many more in sympathy with its working principles and its general position.

I ask in the name of the natural constituency of the Seminary, among the young men in our colleges and churches, whose decision touching Andover awaits your decision.

And yet, even in behalf of these interests, no more than in behalf of my own, do I dare to ask for charity; for I have learned to believe that when great interests are at issue between man and man, and the hearts of men are quick, the fairest thing on the face of the earth in the eyes of all, is justice unadorned.

STATEMENT OF PROFESSOR GEORGE HARRIS.

May it please your Reverend and Honorable Body:

MY object in addressing you is to explain in part my reasons for assenting to the Seminary Creed when I was inaugurated in 1883, with my reasons for continuing to assent to it, and to add a correction of certain misapprehensions which appear to exist relative to the doctrine of Atonement as it is discussed in Progressive Orthodoxy. As I first took the Creed after the present theological controversy began my relation to it was assumed at the outset in the full light of nearly all the objections which have been urged during this hearing.

When it was proposed to me to become Abbot Professor of Christian Theology in the Seminary, I was engaged in the active duties of the pastorate in Providence and had no intention of changing either the form or the place of my Christian service. I was acquainted with the issues which had been raised by the election of Rev. Newman Smyth to the same professorship, but had not made a thorough examination of the Andover Creed. Before the Trustees took action I studied the Creed and Statutes with more carefulness. When I began this study I was by no means confident that I could give a sincere assent to them nor was I certain that I could subscribe to the Westminster Shorter Catechism with the qualifications of the Creed, as the Abbot Professor is required to do. My attention was first given to the doctrines which are now considered most important and concerning which wide differences of opinion prevail, — the doctrines of the Bible, the Person and Work of Christ, and Eschatology. I was at once favorably impressed with the breadth of statement on these doctrines. Great facts are given but no specific theories are proposed. For example I found that the Creed goes no farther than to indicate the religious function of the Bible and that it distinguishes the Word of God from the Scriptures or writings which contain it. Although I held that every part of the Scriptures in connection with the whole is vitally related to the Divine Revelation it conveys, yet it was at once evident that no theory of a verbally inspired or of an infallible Book free from imperfections in every respect could be required. The Word of God is not the very same thing with the *words* of men into which it has been expressed. I saw that the doctrine of the Creed is identical with the doctrine of Paul as stated to Timothy. "Every Scripture inspired of God is also profitable for teaching, for reproof, for correction, for instruction which is in righteousness; that the man of God may be complete, furnished completely unto every good work." The field of fact is left open to inquiry in order that investigation may discover the relation of divine and human elements in the Sacred Scriptures.

The doctrine of the Person of Christ I found expressed in the well-known and generally accepted statement of the Symbol of Chalcedon than which a better formula has not been framed concerning the fact of the union of two natures in one person. The union of divine and human in Christ is generally admitted to present the most difficult problem of theology, and when I heard one of the complainants arguing that problem as against our views in thirteen propositions I entertained for the moment the pious wish of one of the scholars of the Reformation who near the end of his life said that he should welcome a change of worlds for two reasons, one that he might comprehend the union of the two natures, the other that he might be delivered, to use his very language, from the *rabies theologorum*.

The doctrine of Atonement I could not fail to see is stated in a general form and with complete reserve as to what is called the philosophy of Atonement. It emphasizes the fact, the object, and the extent of Atonement made by the sufferings and death of Christ, but the only approach to a theory is the declaration that Christ exercised the priestly office.

The doctrine of Eschatology, as stated in the Creed presented no difficulty except that the language in which the fate of the wicked is described I found to be somewhat more expressive of physical suffering than other Scriptural language which I myself should have selected to express the same belief; namely, the final and irreversible doom of those who are incorrigibly wicked. I assumed that the framers of the Creed held opinions on that subject somewhat more materialistic than the opinions which are held at present. At that time, as I have already stated in my testimony, I had reached no settled conclusion concerning God's dealing with those to whom the gospel is not presented. It then seemed to me that the Scriptures touch that question only incidentally, and that they give no unmistakable utterance. I had, as Bushnell used to put it, hung the question up in my mind. I did not, however, discover that the Creed required one to hold the distinct opinion that no person who is deprived in this life of the ordinary means of grace can have any other opportunity of salvation. The Creed seemed to me to be treating Eschatology and all other doctrines on the basis of a received gospel and of man's duty and destiny in view of the fact that he has the gospel. Although I had not then accepted the opinion for which I am now blamed I did not understand that I must definitely reject it. One, that is, could at least be Agnostic concerning the intermediate state of those who do not have the gospel, since the Creed says nothing about it. If I had then known what I now understand to be the opinion of my colleague in the Stone professorship, which amounts to a confession of ignorance on the subject, I should not have supposed that the Creed requires him to go farther than that. If the Creed obliges one to hold an absolute and exhaustive negative concerning God's dealing with heathen nations I could not have assented to it, nor could I now. I understand my accusers to maintain that the Creed imposes the opinion that for all human beings without any exception whatever there is no opportunity of salvation but that which is given in the earthly life. I should not have dreamed of ascertaining the relation of the Creed to the possibility of Christian probation for the heathen by surmising what the Founders *would* have thought *if* the question had been presented to them. I think there would have been a variety of answers, and that some of them would have said they did not know. I supposed that the only proper course is to bring given opinions concerning which the Creed is silent into the light of the principles or essential doctrines of the Creed, and in such a relation to reach, if it were possible, a conclusion. I turned to the Catechism, which as some have held, dominates the Creed, and discovered that it is entirely silent concerning the fate of the wicked, even of those who do have the gospel. I also believed, as I subsequently declared to the Visitors, that under the Creed there is liberty to hold the opinion that those who do not have the gospel in this life may have it in the life to come. I was also aware that their decision in the case of Rev. Newman Smyth covered this opinion. I had never believed that any man has a second probation under the gospel, and in this respect agreed heartily with the opinions of the Founders — as I do now.

I then turned to other portions of the Creed concerning original sin, election, natural ability, the covenants, etc. It was not till then that difficulties arose. As a theory of moral heredity the doctrine of Federal Headship was repugnant to me. The distinctions of natural and moral ability seemed to me metaphysical refinements, to which I did not care to commit myself, although my judgment of them is now more favorable. These and kindred clauses pertaining to man, and not the clauses which embody revealed truth concerning God, were to me the defective portions of the Creed. It was not the theology, but the psychology and anthropology of the Creed before which I hesitated. I remembered indeed that the only instructor in theology I ever had, my distinguished predecessor in the Abbot professorship, who, as I knew, had had long practice in taking this very Creed, I remembered that he poured derision and ridicule on the doctrine of Federal Headship, and that he declared the covenants of grace and redemption to be figurative and poetical expressions, in order to reach the conclusion that no objection could be made against a figure of speech. Still, I must decide for myself, and at length I reached the conclusion of common sense, that these statements stand for essential facts and doctrines; that Federal Headship signifies the doctrine of depravity and moral heredity as including the entire race, that theories of ability and inability signify man's responsibility and opportunity under the gospel, that the doctrine of election signifies that the individual's confidence of salvation does not rest merely on his own purpose of yesterday, and that it is certain God will redeem to himself a holy people; and all of these opinions were real to me. That is to say, I accepted the substance of doctrine represented by these statements, a substance which in several cases was to me so vital and solid, that in comparison the statements of the Creed seemed to be but the shadow. I felt, sir, as it is said some of the Puritans who lived before the Westminster Confession was framed felt with regard to the phrases of the thirty-nine articles which they considered too lax, that I could take these inadequate statements of the Creed with "a godly interpretation." However, I could not be entirely satisfied without submitting my difficulties to the Board of Visitors, and having the benefit of their advice and judgment. The result was an agreement that the Creed should be taken as expressing substantially the system of truth taught in the Holy Scriptures.

It is noticeable, gentlemen, that the charges most urgently pressed by the complainants do not touch opinions which are covered by specific and clear statements of the Creed, but only opinions concerning doctrines which the Creed introduces in the most general terms. The weight of this accusation bears on our views of the Bible, Atonement, and Eschatology concerning which the Creed is indefinite and reserved. At other points it would have been much easier to argue disagreement. That is to say, the doctrines selected are those which happen just at present to be most in dispute, and it is evident we are opposed not so much because on these doctrines we are antagonistic to the Creed, but rather because our opinions differ from the opinions of our accusers. Such difference we do not for a moment deny.

After my confirmation by your Board, the Creed passed almost entirely out of my thoughts. I remained through the winter with my parish, and at the end of four months was dismissed by Council. Then followed the preparation of an Inaugural address, the fitting up of a house at Andover, and also a growing and appalling sense of what I had undertaken as a teacher of Christian theology. I confess to you, sir, that at times I was profoundly thankful that the Seminary was reduced in numbers and that my first year's course would be heard by only a handful of students.

In addition to the heavy burdens which, as I often felt, I had unwisely assumed, I was made aware at the time of my inauguration of conditions which would make my work still more arduous. It then appeared, in the discussions of the only public and regularly called meeting of the Alumni which within the last four years has considered the theological status of the Seminary, that a determined opposition was to be expected. It was not known that any of the new professors, or indeed that any member of the entire faculty, save one, entertained hope for the unevangelized heathen. But we were not even to have a fair opportunity to prove ourselves. The impressions I then received from intimations and public threats have been abundantly verified. There have been petty insinuations, and constructions offered which if they were not misrepresentations were astonishing misunderstandings. The Seminary was few in numbers as we took it from a former administration, and we had no expectation, with so many untried teachers, of large additions at the outset, yet a journal edited by one of the complainants condescended to make a calculation which by reckoning in lecturers, retired professors, and even the librarian, showed that to each instructor in Andover Seminary there was in attendance one student and five-sevenths of a student. Although our growth has not been rapid, for no efforts have been spared publicly or privately to turn students away from us, similar calculations were not made last year, nor has there been any intimation from that quarter of the considerable growth which the Seminary has had. I have been tempted, and have sometimes yielded to the temptation, to review every sentence of mine which would be printed to ascertain if by any possibility the opponents of the Seminary could construe it to our disadvantage. I have not dared at times (I may have been too timid) to trust an article as a whole, and have modified or omitted sentences which had, as I thought, some point, lest advantage should be taken of a turn of expression. Possibly some of the vagueness of which my accusers complain may be due to such revisions.

I mention all this as part of my experience in the Seminary, and to remind you that opposition did not begin with the appearance of Progressive Orthodoxy in 1885, nor with articles in the "Andover Review" for April and May 1886.

During the last five months I have become better informed in respect to the circumstances under which the Seminary Creed was formulated, and as must be true of all in attendance, I also have learned during the progress of this hearing not a little that was not known before. I have learned from the paper read Friday by Dr. Dexter, or rather have had new illustrations of the fact, that the founders had in view the condition and destiny of men in Christendom, under the gospel. I also judge from that paper that the motive of fear was then worked in too large as it now is worked, according to my judgment, in too small proportion. It has also been made clear to me that the original union included parties which differed as widely as our accusers differ from ourselves. The difference was perhaps even wider, for universality of Atonement as against limitation, and free agency as against inability meant at the time and still mean contrasts as great as any which exist in this present controversy. I have learned that the founders and their friends drove in chaises, wrote precisely worded letters, were not above some log-rolling, tried to influence one man through another man, to get at merchants of Newburyport through their minister, that they suspected the motives of opponents and used rather harsh language towards them, that they were men of like passions with ourselves, that there was more of what we call human nature in them than in their Creed, but also that they were eager for union and were willing to make proper concessions, that they had for their time remarkable breadth of view, above all that they had the courage to put vital principles, of the consequences of which they were not afraid, into their union creed. They did not, I believe, understand how much is involved in the universality of the person and atonement of Christ, nor in the freedom and rationality of man in accordance with which he is saved or lost. But they ventured out. Those principles and doctrines of revelation gained a place in the Creed. They did not know, we do not know, how large results are involved in those truths of Divine revelation. And the fact has been that while some of their statements about man have lost in importance, till they seem to us an almost outgrown metaphysic and ethic, the revealed truths concerning God and his ways with man, which are higher than our thoughts, have enlarged in the apprehension of their descendants and are to enlarge more and more by reverent study of God's works in creation, providence and redemption, by clearer knowledge of the Bible, and by the deepening spiritual experience which believers gain in their "minds and hearts."

I have also examined the relation of Creed and Catechism, a relation in which I am the only living person who has a directly responsible interest, and have come to a conclusion which I believe to have been expressed by my predecessor, that in the case of the Abbot Professor a legal reference to the Catechism is appropriate, but that the Creed determines the sense in which those portions of the Catechism shall be taken which are found in both instruments. I am not able to understand the satisfaction my colleagues on the Associate foundation take in their freedom from the Catechism, even as interpreted by the Creed, for with the exception of the doctrine of limited atonement, which the Creed corrects, I consider the Westminster Catechism, as a doctrinal formulary, superior to the Andover Creed.

One point has perhaps been overlooked by the complainants.

The Catechism teaches that the world was made in the space of six days. There is no doubt in my mind that the Westminster Divines meant by that 144 hours. The statement is not modified by the Creed. But I do not believe that the world was created in six solar days. I believe that the universe was created in no time. As Augustine said, the world was not created *in tempore*, but *cum tempore*. Or, if by creation is meant the time from the appearance of matter to the appearance of man, I should prefer to assume millions rather than even thousands of years. Nor have we yet done with the consequences which come in with a recognition of the time required for the evolution of the existing order, since this change of opinion may prove to involve essential doctrines.

We may expect our accusers next to turn their attention to the Presbyterian body, for the clergymen and theological professors of that denomination take the Catechism without the modifications of a later Creed, yet many of them hold to the universality of atonement.

On the whole, more careful study of the origin of the Creed, to which this trial has invited me has not substantially changed my understanding of it. Neither have my opinions substantially changed. I have not, let me hope, stopped thinking, even if premiums have been offered to encourage cessation of thought. Neither, let me also hope, have I ceased to receive the light which God gives to those who honestly seek the truth. My changes of doctrinal view have been in respect to proportion, emphasis and clearness. I do find it easier to reconcile the significance and scope of atonement with the opinion that the knowledge of it will be given to all men before the final judgment than with the opinion that the light of nature is essentially the knowledge of Christ, or with the opinion that all knowledge of God in Christ, except that which is given in this life, is withheld from the perishing heathen. My difficulty, sir, is with the alternatives. I only say that upon the hypothesis which I entertain some serious objections disappear, and that it harmonizes certain essential doctrines of the gospel with the Providence of God, but that it is of secondary rather than primary value, in the sense that it is an inference from essential doctrines rather than itself an essential doctrine. I would also say that if the Creed requires me to hold definitely that no member of the unevangelized nations has other knowledge of God for his salvation than that which he gains in this life, I desire to be emancipated from such a creed at the earliest possible moment. But I do not interpret your former decision as shutting one up to such a conclusion. I understand that the Creed requires no more than the essentials of faith as given in other evangelical symbols. In our own denomination, council after council has decided that the opinion I hold on the probation of the heathen does not override any essential article of faith.

The most serious charge which has been brought against me is in my judgment to my opinions on the Atonement. The gospel in its very essence is the redemption of sinful man through Jesus Christ, and to be in error concerning it is more reprehensible than to believe that the Bible contains some blemishes incidental to the human media through which its truth was given, or to hold a certain opinion concerning God's grace to the heathen. I do not propose to discuss the doctrine but to correct some misapprehensions. As I listened to the paper which was devoted chiefly to that topic, I perceived that while it condemned my view it indicated the view, and apparently the only view which the writer considers correct, or tenable under the Creed. I observed that he understands the Creed to be committed to the so-called governmental theory of Atonement. As the reading proceeded, the ideas presented, the expressions used, the turns given to phrases, the repetition of favorite words were such that if the voice had not been different and I had closed my eyes I should have believed myself to be back again where I was nearly a score of years ago in the middle class lecture-room at Andover listening to the Abbot Professor of Theology as he gave his interesting expositions of the Grotian theory of Atonement. Now I believe that theory to be permissible under the Creed, although to my thinking, since it finds the principal effect of Atonement in the exhibition it makes to sinners and to the universe of God's regard for his law, it is in the last analysis, a moral influence theory.

But I call attention to the fact that whatever is true in the Grotian or governmental theory of Atonement is included in the presentation of the subject in Progressive Orthodoxy. It is stated on page 57 that the sufferings and death of Christ realize God's hatred of sin and the righteous authority of law, and that therefore punishment need not be exacted. This line of reflection was not followed out because, as stated in the article, it is so familiar. "Its meaning is" says the book "that God cannot be regardless of law nor indifferent to sin in saving man from punishment." That is the pith of the governmental theory. Then comes the passage urged so emphatically in the complaint. "It must be confessed that it is not clear how the sufferings and death of Christ can be substituted for the punishment of sin" (but we have not reached the end of the sentence) "how because Christ made vivid the wickedness of sin and the righteousness of God, man is therefore any the less exposed to the consequences of sin. We must go on to the fact that Christ makes real *very much more* than God's righteous indignation against sin. The punishment of sin does not save men. It only vindicates God and his law. Christ while declaring God's righteousness reveals God seeking men at the cost of sacrifice." It is not the error but the inadequacy of the governmental 'theory which is criticised.

The entire discussion is on the basis of propitiation. The fundamental position is that because God is reconciled to man therefore man is forgiven, rather than that God forgives by reason of any thing that man does. First God is reconciled, then man repents. Not first man repents and then God is reconciled. Much space is given to an inquiry concerning the offering which humanity makes to God in the sacrifice of Christ. I quote — "Humanity may thus be thought of as offering something to God of eminent value. When Christ suffers the race suffers. When Christ is sorrowful the race is sorrowful." Why did Dr. Wellman's quotation stop here? Let us go on. "Christ realizes what humanity could not realize for itself. The race may be conceived as approaching God, and signifying its penitence by pointing to Christ, and by giving expression in him to repentance which no words could utter." And then with but a sentence between comes this statement. "The representative power which belongs to man in his various relations comes to its perfect realization in Christ. In the family, in government, in business, in society, representative or substitutionary relations are the rule not the exception. Much more has Christ the power perfectly to represent us or to be substituted for us, because there is no point of our real life where he is not in contact with us."

But the most singular part of the objection is the criticism made on my belief in the union of Christ with the race. Because the Incarnation, which is the true humanity of Christ, helps us to understand the Atonement, it is concluded that Incarnation has been put in the place of Atonement. The article was endeavoring to express the opinion that Christ's union with the race gives large part of its significance to his sufferings and death. "For verily not of angels doth he take hold, but he taketh hold of the seed of Abraham. Wherefore it behooved him in all things to be made like unto his brethren that he might be a merciful and faithful high priest in things pertaining to God to make propitiation for the sins of the people." The fact that Christ in his incarnation became a real man in organic relation with the human race gives the most profound conception of his Atonement. It should also be observed that in the statement concerning incarnation it is perfectly clear that something other is meant than the completed union of Christ with the believer. And this view of Christ's proper humanity is argued to be in opposition to the statement of the Creed that Jesus Christ and he *alone* made atonement for the sins of all men; as if "alone" means that he has no organic union with the men for whom he laid down his life. This is as complete a reversal of an author's meaning as it was ever my misfortune to hear. I believe the framers of the Creed were not desirous of propounding any *theory* of Atonement but of emphasizing its extent.

In a similar vein the opinions presented on man's power to repent were discussed. There is, in the article cited, an inquiry concerning fact, concerning man's real rather than his formal freedom. The word "cannot" is Paul's "cannot" when he said, "I cannot do the things which I would." I understood that the view we are required to hold under the creed, in the opinion of our accusers, is that man does all of his repenting by his own unaided power and that after he has achieved a complete repentance, God forgives him on account of the sacrifice of Christ. I had supposed that man does his sinning by his own unaided power, but that when it comes to holiness, especially that radical choice in which real repentance largely consists and which is a true turning to God, he is to no small degree dependent on the Holy Spirit of God taking the things of Christ and showing them unto him. In that opinion I believe I am in most substantial accord with the Seminary Creed.

Some of these speculations to which we have listened made the impression on me that it is extremely difficult for what may be called the logical school of evangelical belief to enter into a sympathetic appreciation of the beliefs of the spiritual school. I am prepared to abate somewhat the feeling that our accusers and their associates *refuse* to understand us as we mean, for it has been borne in on me during this hearing that they probably are *unable* so to understand us — I do not intend this observation as a slur, but as the statement of a fact. I do not deny that our writings may sometimes have been vague. But I am satisfied that the real difficulty lies deeper, and that the two parties or wings are separated somewhat as parties in the church have been separated in almost every period of its history — because they approach truth from opposite sides, or rather because the one party approaches from without on the circumference, the other party from within at or near the centre. This difference is partly constitutional and so cannot be avoided. It is a remark made first

I think by Schelling, although attributed to Coleridge, that every man as to philosophy is born either a Platonist or Aristotelian. It is equally true that as to theology some men are endowed with spiritual, others more largely with logical apprehension. It seems to me that our opponents almost completely fail to apprehend that movement of religious thought of the last thirty years in this and other countries which has been the advancing supremacy of the rational, ethical and spiritual habit of thought in place of a syllogistic, logical and therefore rationalizing habit. If I had time, sir, I should like to maintain that the later developments of New England theology have been more rationalistic than any theological movement since the Scholastic period.

If I may be pardoned a generalization without prefatory discussion I should say that one school of thought looks at truth in its objective forms as an external thing, that the re-action is mysticism which evolves beliefs out of subjective feeling, and that the newer school of thought in our own time appropriates external truth by reason and spirit into living faiths, uniting the objective and subjective. Whenever these contrasted parties have been contemporaneous it has been easier for the spiritual or intuitional school to comprehend the merely logical than for the logical to comprehend the spiritual. Paul understands James better than James understands Paul. John understands Peter better than Peter understands John. But it is easier for the logical than for the other school to state its opinions clearly and to defend them adroitly. The Anselmic (at least as it is frequently stated) and the Grotian theories of Atonement, for example, can be put in a nutshell and made intelligible to any one, and that is the trouble with them. They make Atonement a device and do not see that it is God seeking men. Now, not to dwell on this distinction, what is true in other denominations is true in ours that one party is moved on by the deeper currents of rational and spiritual impulse while the other does not escape the syllogistic and formal methods to which it has become accustomed. These are the differences which confront us at this trial.

That which to the one school is the vital, organic, real relation of Christ to men is to the other school mysticism and vagueness.

The complainants will say that this very state of things is fatal to us for the admission is made that we are on another track than that on which all Christians travelled at the beginning of this century. But, on the contrary, I contend that the two parties which entered into this union were really unlike in these very respects. On the one side were mechanical, artificial opinions concerning imputation, representation, Divine Sovereignty; on the other side were character in freedom, an organic relation of man to man, and of man to Christ, and a purpose of God running through history and revealing him as the God of reason and love. Then as now, and as always, there were the contrasts of legal and spiritual, external and internal, conservative and progressive, old and new. Since the beginning there have been alternations in the teachings at Andover. Much of the time both schools have been represented. Both schools are represented there to-day. It is doubtless well for the church and the world that both types of thought exist and, to some degree, work harmoniously side by side. The fruitfulness of the great truths of revelation and of the advancing kingdom of Christ produces various types. The doctrinal Paul, the mystical John, the ecclesiastical James are reflected and reproduced in all the great bodies of Christendom. If the tenure of either party under the Creed is in doubt it is of that party which to-day opposes us, since the Creed crowded hard on formal views of the external relations of men to each other and to Christ. We should claim that we are more nearly in the line of that vigorous movement which enlarged the old faith into new meaning and scope. But the Seminary Creed was then and is still a platform for the two principal schools of evangelical faith.

In my judgment the particular opinion which is held of the opportunities of heathen men is of less importance than that there be a firm hold on those great postulates of the gospel's truth from which we think our theory properly proceeds. I could not as I have said assent to the Creed if it compels me to maintain a negative concerning the unevangelized nations, much less if it shuts me up to theories of Atonement and of the Bible which have been represented here as alternative to my own. I had supposed that Andover with its origin, history and traditions is a good institution for the advancement of Christian doctrine. But if I must try to squeeze my opinions into any given phraseology and to institute at every point a microscopic comparison with the Creed I should decline thus to sacrifice spontaneity, enthusiasm and progress. You very well know that none of us care for the salaries we receive since every one of us remains at Andover at a pecuniary sacrifice, but we do care for the advantage of our positions to advance the gospel of Christ, and we do care for saving the institution to its intended uses. It was not established as an asylum for orthodoxy, but as a school for "increasing the number of learned and able Defenders of the Gospel of Christ, as well as of orthodox, pious, and zealous Ministers of the New Testament"; for the production of character and influence devoted to the service of Christ.

I beg only, in addition, to call your attention to a phrase in the Statutes which has been misapplied. Emphasis has been laid on the direction that the Creed should never be altered in any particular. But it never has been altered. It is identically the same as at the first. The intention was to prevent the Trustees or Visitors from repealing any clauses, or adding new clauses. There was to be no more legislation on that subject. It was rather a safeguard against retrogression than a bar to advance. The true inference from that provision is that there is all the more reason for allowing a liberal and Christian construction of a Creed which is itself forever unchangeable.

STATEMENT OF PROFESSOR EDWARD Y. HINCKS.

THE work assigned to me by the Trustees of Andover Seminary with the concurrence of your honorable Body, is that of interpreting the Scriptures. This task of interpretation includes not only the correct rendering of the words of the inspired writers, but the tracing out of their leading thoughts, and their subordinate ideas in their connection with these. It also includes such discussion of the historical questions pertaining to the respective date, authorship, and immediate purpose of the Sacred writings as is essential to a correct understanding of their contents. In doing this work I have tried to be true to the province required of me by the constituted authorities of the Seminary "to open and explain the Scriptures to my pupils with integrity and faithfulness."

I assume that an honest and faithful expositor will try to ascertain as nearly as possible the meaning of the language used by the inspired writers, by the use of such grammatical, etymological and illustrative helps as are at his command. I also take for granted that he will try to enter into sympathy as far as possible with the religious feelings and motives which animated these writers. Having done this he will, I likewise assume, declare their thoughts, according to his best understanding of them; not allowing his representations to be modified by his own prejudices or those of others. Such unbiassed interpretation I have tried to give to those of the Scriptures which I have had occasion to expound. In deciding upon the questions involving facts relating to these Scriptures, I have acted upon the principle, that the laws which govern historical research in one field must govern it in every field;

and that problems for which revelation does not furnish means of solution must be solved by strictly historical methods.

At the same time these principles of interpretation and research have been employed under the avowed conviction that the Scriptures are a supernaturally given source of spiritual enlightenment and carry the absolute authority of the Divine Redeemer. I have endeavored to show that the divine communications made to our Lord and his apostles, and those given to the ancient prophets have passed over into them and make them the prime source of religious knowledge, and the final test of Christian belief.

If I have not claimed for them perfect accuracy in all statements lying outside of the sphere of religious truth, and if I have assigned to them functions of varying value in revealing God's character and ways, it is because this is necessarily involved in showing the connection with Christ in the light of which alone their authority can be appreciated and their meaning understood. Since God's revelation to man centres in Him, all parts of that revelation must be seen as related to that centre to be understood. This implies the historical study of Scripture, its examination in the light of contemporaneous facts and events. Such examination implies of course the faithful use of historical methods and the honest recognition of their results. A firm conviction that the Scriptures contain the religious conceptions of Christ and his apostles forbids any shrinking from such candid research. The wish to keep that conviction fresh is an unceasing stimulus to pursue it. I may remind you that to this part of the work of a Biblical teacher in Andover Seminary great importance was attached by its Founders as appears from Article VI. of the original constitution, which I beg permission to read.

Article VI. Under the head of Sacred Literature shall be included Lectures on the formation, preservation and transmission of the Sacred Volume; on the languages in which the Bible was originally written; on the Septuagint version of the Old Testament and on the peculiarities of the language and style of the New Testament, resulting from this version and other causes; on the history character use and authority of the ancient version of the Old and New Testaments; on the canons of Biblical criticism; on the authenticity of the several books of the sacred Code; on the apocryphal books of both Testaments; on modern translations of the Bible, more particularly on the history and character of our English version; and also critical Lectures on the various readings and difficult passages in the sacred writings.

While I have aimed to present the Scriptures in their historical and living connection with Christ, and thus to establish for them a higher value than such as comes from a purely formal authority, I have never reached conclusions as regards their nature or their teachings at variance with the Creed or any of the Christian doctrines expressed in it. I desire at this point in behalf of my associates and myself to correct representations made by one of the Complainants in his plea, of the meaning of certain cited passages from the articles on the Scriptures submitted as evidence by the prosecution.

From the editorial entitled " The Bible a Theme for the Pulpit" the following sentence (And. Rev. v. 409) was quoted by him as proof that the article advocates a covert opposition to the orthodox doctrine of inspiration, on the part of ministers. " A minister who should begin to preach a series of sermons about the Bible by saying that he expected to show that the notion of inspiration in which his hearers had been trained was an erroneous one, would probably find a considerable part of his congregation resolutely opposed to his teaching from the outset." To this I would add the sentence which follows — "The misunderstanding as to his conception of the Bible created by his injudicious remark — (injudicious because misrepresenting the real nature of the proposed teaching), could hardly be removed by any subsequent explanations." It is here plainly implied that the teaching suggested is not really at variance with the evangelical view of the Scriptures.

The following sentences which I will not stay to cite make the implication yet more evident. I will add a word, explaining another sentence from this editorial discussed by the same gentleman, "Then, as inspired life is shown expressing itself in inspired teaching, — as for example the connection between Paul's written teaching and his own inner life and his apostolic work is traced, or the apostolic tradition is shown embodying itself in the Synoptic Gospels — the conviction will gradually be created that the Scripture is the vehicle by which the divine revelation is conveyed to men, and in no true sense the revelation itself." The word "revelation" is used here in its Scriptural sense, of a supernatural disclosure of truth to inspired teachers. Paul e.g. says in the Epistle to the Galatians that God revealed his Son in him that he might preach Him. Paul's epistles bring the revelation which he received to us. They are not the revelation itself, for it expressed itself in them. There are important ends, it is thought, in pointing out the distinction. The charge that it is derogatory to the Scriptures is as absurd as would be the claim that one depreciated Christ's parables in saying that they were the vehicle by which his ideas were conveyed to the mind of the people. I must also correct the same gentleman's interpretation of a sentence belonging to the article on the Scriptures in "Progressive Orthodoxy" (p. 221). "We are finding out that the seat of the prophetic teaching was the moral and religious nature of the inspired seer alone." It was elaborately urged that this refers the teaching of the prophets to a purely human source. Indeed the word source was used as a synonym for "seat" in interpreting the sentence. But the claim could hardly have been made if the sentence had been read in its context. For it is preceded by these words.

"That conception of the prophet which regarded him as merely a voice, uttering words which his own inner life had no share in producing is rapidly disappearing before the intelligent study of the Old Testament." And we pass over but one sentence to come to these words . . . "It is not denied that they were sometimes evidently conscious of receiving special messages from God. Nor would we claim that the conceptions of God's kingdom in its present state and coming development, given them by the Spirit, were so thoroughly wrought into their own thinking as the apostles' conceptions of Christ and his Kingdom were united with their own thought."

One more instance of misrepresentation in the use of the same article must be pointed out. The following words are found on page 231.

"Whatever else comes to us as from God must present its credentials to Christ's truth in our minds and hearts."

These last words, it is said, show that the writer recognized no objective divine revelation. But let me read the context.

"If Christ is the supreme and final Revelation, He is the test of all preceding revelation. If we accept Him as God's supreme and final revelation, we must bring preceding revelation to this test. We cannot escape the process of comparison if we would. He brings us his own conception of God, of life, of duty. It claims to cover the whole horizon of truth, and demands possession of every spiritual and rational faculty. If we will have it as ours we must hold it separate from and above every other. Whatever else comes to us as from God must present its credentials to Christ's truth in our minds and hearts."

The two last sentences are evidently to be read in close connection. Their obvious meaning is that if we will take Christ's truth into our hearts we must give it royal authority over them, and make it judge of every thing that claims to come empowered by God to enter them. Not our notions, but Christ's truth within us is to rule our inner being.

The earlier sentences expressly emphasize the supremacy of the objective Christian revelation.

I repeat that I have been both in belief and teaching true to "the principles of the Creed;" to quote words of Professor Stuart cited by the prosecution.

I will frankly admit however my belief that the Creed itself gives me a degree of liberty in interpreting its tenets. In the pledge which it exacts the promise "to open and explain the Scriptures to my pupils with integrity and faithfulness" precedes that "to maintain and inculcate the Christian faith, as expressed in the Creed by me now repeated." That promise has, I conceive, especial force for those who are called to teach the Bible in the Seminary. They at any rate are required by it to make the exposition of the Scriptures "according to the best light God shall give" them, the shaping and paramount principle of their teaching. They are to explain the Bible with integrity; giving no interpretations but such as are the fruit of their own study and research, and carry their own conviction; they are to explain it with faithfulness, counting subservience to human opinion unfaithfulness not only to the Scripture, but to the Seminary which requires a fair exposition of the word of God. This to men who like the Founders, regarded the Bible as the depository of divine truth must have implied the expectation of a progressive unfolding of that truth on the part of the teachers of sacred literature. It would have been absurd to require a promise to "open and expound the Scriptures with integrity and faithfulness," if the conclusions reached were expected to be absolutely identical with those already arrived at and set forth. Indeed, the word "open" seems to imply an advance into undeveloped riches of divine truth.

If I am correct in believing that the Founders laid this promise of a progressive teaching of Scripture upon the Biblical teachers in the Seminary, I may assume that they expected those teachers to interpret the creed in the light of that promise. To claim that they regarded their statement of belief as an absolutely perfect representation of the doctrinal contents of the Bible is to impugn not only their good judgment but their sincerity, since they have put the Scriptures above the creed as "the only perfect rule of faith and practice." To put such an interpretation upon the creed therefore as would prevent the teachers in the Seminary from keeping abreast of contemporaneous Biblical Scholarship by the use of legitimate methods (if such an interpretation were possible) would thwart their wishes both by making the Creed, not the Bible the ultimate test of the teaching of the institution as well as the "only perfect rule" of its professors' belief, and by robbing its Biblical instruction of that manifest and avowed loyalty to the Scriptures as the one unquestionable and paramount authority which the Founders intended it should have.

It is not meant of course, that the several articles of the creed have not a meaning for every one who teaches under it. No one could claim e.g. that one could go on teaching in the Seminary who had become satisfied that the Scriptures furnished no reason for believing in the doctrine of the Trinity. The enactment requiring a renewed subscription at the expiration of each five years;—which recognizes a necessary movement of mind engaged in the study of divine truth, provides that such movement shall be bounded by the great doctrinal lines plainly indicated by the Creed. I for one would not retain my position five years nor one year, had I abandoned any of the doctrines enunciated there. But I do not think retaining it inconsistent with the belief that the Scriptures may yet afford the means of giving one or more of those doctrines a better expression. For I am sure that such Biblical teaching as they exact by solemn pledge implies this belief.

I close by declaring my full and hearty belief "that the word of God, contained in the Scriptures of the Old and New Testament is the only perfect rule of faith and practice," and by denying that I have in the lecture-room or out of it made statements inconsistent with this belief, or inconsistent with my promise to "open and explain the Scriptures to my pupils with integrity and faithfulness," to "maintain and inculcate the Christian faith as expressed in the Creed of the Seminary," together with all the other doctrines and duties of our Holy Religion, so far as may appertain to my office, according to the best light God shall give me."

STATEMENT OF PROFESSOR J. W. CHURCHILL.

May it please your Reverend and Honorable Board: —

IN filing my exception to the charges against me for holding, maintaining, and inculcating opinions that are contrary to the Associate Creed of Andover Theological Seminary, I desire that it be understood as explicitly as language can express my position that I am not seeking to evade in the slightest degree my share of the editorial responsibility in the purpose and conduct of "The Andover Review;" or to avoid whatsoever consequences may follow from an adverse decision against my co-editors upon the citations from the Review as evidence of teaching and maintaining opinions in nonconformity to the Seminary Creed. The fate of one editor is the fate of all the editors. Nor do I wish to suggest the inference that I am not in perfect sympathy with the spirit and aim that animate and control the movement and tendency in contemporary religious thought known as Progressive Orthodoxy. I adhere to the principles of the movement, although I do not accept every inference from some of its positions. Neither let it be inferred that I consider my adherence to Progressive Orthodoxy as inimical to the Associate Creed, which I conscientiously subscribed to on my inauguration into the Jones Professorship of Elocution, which I have since twice repeated as an act of solemn obligation in the presence of the Trustees of the Seminary, and to which I am still loyal as it has been interpreted and administered for more than half a century. Nor do I desire, in filing this exception, to add to the already numerous complications of this perplexing public Inquiry into the Orthodoxy of the editors of "The Andover Review." Much less do I wish to embarrass your reverend and honorable Board with untimely or irrelevant demands upon your attention. Still less would I convey the impression that I do not wish, or that I ought not, to be placed under your supervision, or that I resist any claim that your reverend and honorable Body may lawfully make for its Visitorial jurisdiction over the Jones Professorship.

But the question occasionally has been discussed in high quarters, and especially during the last few months, whether or not the Jones Professorship is strictly under the control of the Visitors of the Associate Foundation. In the Statutes of the various Chairs of Instruction that have been founded since the establishment of the Associate Creed, there seem to be three classes of conditions: one class, represented by the Taylor Professorship of Biblical Theology and History, now held by Professor Taylor, distinctly places the chair under the Visitorial supervision of your reverend and honorable Board; a second class, represented by the Stone Professorship of the Relations of Christianity to the Secular Sciences, now held by Professor Gulliver, distinctly states the exemption of the chair from your Visitorial control; the third class, represented by the Jones Professorship of Elocution, makes no reference whatsoever to the relation of the chair to any Visitorial supervision.

It is for the sole purpose of permanently determining the question of your Visitorial relation to the Jones Professorship that I filed my eleventh exception. I have availed myself of the occasion of this trial to submit the test; because, if the Jones Professorship is not under your Visitorial jurisdiction, then the complainants have no case against me upon which your reverend and honorable Board can adjudicate; if, on the other hand, it shall be decided that the Jones Professorship is under your Visitorial supervision, I shall cheerfully conform to your requirements in the premises, and shall respond to the charges preferred against me in such a manner as your Board shall direct.

Since it has been determined that it is advisable for me to make a statement in connection with the statements of my colleagues, I have thrown together this morning the few expressions following that partially may answer the present purpose of meeting the charges preferred against me.

It will be remembered by your reverend and honorable Board that in reply to your requisition of July 27, 1886, to present a written answer to the original charges within fifteen days that I conformed to your requirements within a very few days after the allotted time. The reply was made before the indicted professors had engaged counsel to defend them; but this fact was overlooked, inadvertently, I am willing to believe, in the counsel's argument for the prosecution in the case of my colleague, Professor Smyth, and through the omission an erroneous and injurious impression must have been conveyed to you and to the public concerning our action in the early history of this case.

You will also recall the fact that, in answer to the Amended Charges, there was presented to you a written reply from each of my colleagues, and that no reply was sent in by me, but that I added to the general Bill of Exceptions a special exception claiming that my Professorship was not under your jurisdiction. I withheld my answer to the Amended Charges until I should learn your decision on the point in question. Had I received the decision before this Court opened the case of Professor Smyth I should have sent in my written reply couched in the same language that was employed in the replies of my colleagues. I should also have prepared a more complete and careful statement than this, and of a different character, to meet the demands of the present time and place. But, inasmuch as no decision has been rendered upon my special exception, and also for the sake of brevity, I ask permission of your reverend and honorable Board to refer to the answer of my colleagues as being identical with my own; since what was common to those answers is expressed in the same language, and was discussed and drawn up in my presence, and with my voluntary co-operation as being equally indicted with them.

I would also respectfully ask permission, under the circumstances, to refer for ampler defence to the exposition of the

Seminary Creed as given by the Rev. D. T. Fiske, D.D., the venerable and honored President of the Board of Trustees of Andover Theological Seminary. I doubt not that I can safely rely upon your familiarity with that document. My intellectual and moral attitude towards the Creed is exactly defined in Dr. Fiske's Exposition. The high character, theological attainments, wisely conservative temper, and candid spirit of Dr. Fiske, are a sufficient guaranty to me of a competent and accurate representation of the Creed in his account of its origin, its subsequent history, its character, the significance of subscription to it, the history of its administration, and the source of responsibility in deciding the orthodoxy of the Professor in relation to the Creed. I refer to Dr. Fiske's Exposition and rely upon it, because its original intention was neither polemical in tone, nor inimical in its spirit towards any individual connected with the Board of Instruction or of Administration. It was not written for any Starchamber assembly in secret conclave with the purpose of ultimately making it an iron heel to crush the advocate of some obnoxious doctrine: it was written solely for the information of the North Essex Ministerial Association with which he is connected, and with no intention of subsequent publication. Dr. Fiske's paper was entirely successful in removing previous unfortunate misconceptions, and conveyed much valuable information to his ministerial associates. That accomplished theologian, the late Rev. Raymond H. Seeley, D.D., of Haverhill, gave it his cordial endorsement. The Exposition afforded such general satisfaction that it was published at the request of the Association. The Rev. Ray Palmer, D.D., a former Visitor of the Seminary, has declared Dr. Fiske's Essay to be "a fair and honest statement of the essential facts of the case, and well adapted to set the public — those who *wish* to be set right — in a position to judge of the whole matter." He affirms that the view of the Creed, so clearly and ably presented, and the meaning of subscription to it was that which he himself entertained when he subscribed to it. "It was that," he adds, "of Drs. Dwight and Smith when they became Visitors." (See Prefatory Note to Dr.

Fiske's Exposition: Cupples, Upham & Co., Boston, Dec. 17, 1886.)

Upon my election to office in the Seminary I consulted my honored professor of Sacred Rhetoric concerning the manner in which the Creed was to be taken, for I had often heard it spoken of as an iron-clad affair of a past age, which had mostly lost its force and was only loosely binding upon the teachers of the present. Professor Phelps answered: " You must take the Creed as the rest of us have taken it — in its historic sense, and for substance of doctrine." His explanation of those terms (which I do not now recall in his language) satisfied me that an honest man could take the Creed honestly; but it also disclosed to me the fact that the Creed required interpretation.

Accepting Dr. Fiske's exposition as my *vade mecum* in the interpretation of the Creed, I affirm my deliberate and conscientious conviction that if the Creed had the inherent power to effect the union of conflicting schools of religious thought in the days of its origin, it has the very same inherent power in the present day to prevent division and separation.

I cannot suppose that my personal views on the Ethics of Creed-Subscription are of the slightest importance to your reverend and Honorable Board. Nevertheless, they are of vital importance to me; and I find myself in such hearty accord with the principles of Creed subscription as enunciated by Professor Austin Phelps, that I venture to make reference to the chapter in one of his works, — "My Portfolio," and entitled the "Rights of Believers in Ancient Creeds." Many of the illustrations in that clear, comprehensive, and conservative discussion are drawn from the Seminary Creed and the history of its administration (see p. 41 *et seq.*). I may safely assume your acquaintance with Professor Phelps's views upon this important topic. I refer to Dr. Fiske and to Professor Phelps as reflecting more perfectly and more vividly my own views, and for the purpose of brevity at this late stage of the proceedings.

In this manner, also, I express my sincere reverence for the framers of the Creed in their strenuous efforts to secure a true expression of theological doctrine. As time goes on, my veneration for those wise and able men is deepened, and my confidence in the greatness of their purpose, and my admiration for their achievement, are confirmed. Their elaborate formulary is not an antiquated relic, but is an impressive and living memorial of their insight into religious Truth, and of their theological prowess. They were guided by the promised Spirit of Truth, who has never been absent from the church in its work of creed-construction, and who is still in the hearts of men that are called upon to interpret the religious symbols of a former time.

I am glad to express my sympathy with the doctrinal conclusions at which they arrived. Every theological and Scriptural *fact* they registered in that Creed is true, and always will be true. Their skill in putting those truths into logical and vital relations is remarkable, and it remains a noble expression of the tenets of consistent Calvinism. But who shall call it a final expression of truth? It contains truth so far as it goes, but it does not exhaust it. Every Creed is a monument of man's imperfection. I believe this Creed, but I never can relinquish my right to think upon theological topics independently of the Creed, and outside of its terms, provided that, in the use of my conclusions, I am not inharmonious with a sound interpretation of the Creed or antagonistic to it. The responsibility of subscription ultimately rests upon the Professor himself. Any man likely to be elected to any chair in the Seminary is supposed to be intelligent and honest enough to decide for himself whether he can or cannot conscientiously subscribe, or maintain his subscription, to the Creed; and no man has a right to go behind the subscriber's conscience, or try to displace it by substituting some other man's interpretation.

In saying this, I mean to imply the inadequacy of this, and any existing Creed, to cover all the subjects of theological inquiry and discussion that constantly emerge in the gradual development of the aspects of Truth. Religion is a life, the life of God in the soul of man; but Theology is the Science of Religion. Theology, with all the sciences, is bound to regard changing data, and constantly must be passed under review for revision and re-adjustment. There is new light in Philosophy, new light in History, new light in Science, new light in Criticism, that is constantly breaking forth. If fresh light in any of these departments of thought and endeavor that are organically related to the facts and truths of theological science can be allowed to flash out in Yale Seminary or in Union, — and it is flashing there — then I want its brightness in Andover, to make the Creed still more an illuminating power; and through Andover to shine in upon the spiritual darkness of the nations. If a narrow construction of the Creed is to act as an extinguisher, or as a minimizing agent in denying me the benefits or the use of any new light, I shall see to it that I do not suffer the condemnation of those who love darkness rather than light.

Wonder has often been expressed that a Professor of Elocution should be accused of heretical teaching of Theology. My offence arises in the fact that I am a responsible co-editor of the heretical "Andover Review." I have already expressed my willingness to share every thing that editorial responsibility carries with it. As editors we work and express ourselves in the plural and not in the singular. In explanation of my arraignment it has been said in pleasantry that I have been indicted for giving to the enunciation of "Sheol" a circumflex inflection as expressing doubt. Not so; on the contrary, and all jesting apart at a time of seriousness, I enunciate "Sheol," and teach my pupils to enunciate it, and every word symbolizing a revealed fact of solemn import, with the firm, downward inflection expressive of the affirmation of the reality of a positive personal conviction. Not one of my colleagues is so poor a theologian or so unskilful a speaker as to confound a downward inflection with a circumflex.

I have not yet found the term "Probation" a necessity for my theology or my view of life, here or hereafter. I do not find it in the Creed, excepting as it refers to Adam's probation in his relation as the federal head of the race; nor is it a biblical word, although the idea is admitted to be scriptural. I have been accustomed to regard this earthly scene and God's relation to it, not as a court-room, nor even a school-room, but as a scene of moral education in which the Father of Spirits is training the nations and individuals composing His great human family for the Eternal Life beyond life. As I think I stated in my former answer to you, I cannot believe that every soul's life in the Fatherhood of God will have its moral discipline ended with its earthly career; but, undoubtedly, there are souls existing both in this world and the next that forever will resist the Divine purpose and means in discipline. But it is not needful that I should enlarge upon this view in order to guard it, or to defend it, or to show its harmony with the Creed. The spiritual results in holy character in the great multitude of the Redeemed in the Eternal World are the same in my view of the future life that the advocates of a continued probation for the mass of the evangelically Unprivileged hope to see gloriously realized.

I know the history of the so-called Andover hypothesis of Continued Probation, from the first syllable of its utterance to the present hour. I have been in most intimate relations, day in and day out, year in and year out, with its supporters. I know a hundred times better than those who have misunderstood and consequently have misrepresented them, the spirit and manner, the limitations, lights and shades, and the conditions of development in which the hypothesis has been maintained. But little value may be attached to a personal opinion; nevertheless, the circumstances of this public statement make it proper for me to say that, inasmuch as I am convinced that this hypothesis does not militate against the doctrines of the Depravity of Man, the Necessity of Regeneration, the Trinity of the Godhead, the Universal Atonement of Christ, or the Eternity of Future Rewards and Punishments, which doctrines are authoritatively declared to be the distinguishing, essential, and pivotal doctrines in the system of Truth which the Seminary Creed, and all the great historic confessions affirm, — therefore, in view of such harmony with these tests of Orthodoxy,

I earnestly claim for my colleagues their liberty of opinion, teaching, and discussion concerning this hypothesis. More than this: I believe that there is Reason and Scripture in it.

In making answer in this special form demanded by the present exigency of the case, I trust that I have again affirmed my sincere, reverent, and hearty loyalty to the elaborate symbol that I am called upon to sign as a Professor in Andover Theological Seminary. Whatsoever minor diversities of formal expression or of individual interpretation my colleagues or myself may demand as our rights as believers in the Creed, I sincerely believe that they are held in accordance with sound and recognized principles of Creed-Subscription. I sincerely believe that such modifications of belief or statement do not impair the integrity of doctrine as expressed in our authoritative standard. They are simply changed aspects of unchangeable truths. I sincerely believe that the intention of the Framers of this Creed was to make forever secure the teaching of a large, an enlarging, and a tolerant Orthodoxy; that they were intent upon making the teaching in the Seminary a synonym for a true, consistent, and catholic theology. Moreover, I sincerely and intelligently affirm that there exists in the religious community a wide-spread and positive judgment, that organized opposition to competent and conscientious teaching on the doctrinal basis laid by the Founders of the Seminary, is inconsistent with a true liberty of teaching within the limits of the Creed; and that such organized opposition is subversive of the stability of true theology,—a permanence that must ever be conditioned upon freedom of theological teaching and discussion as an inalienable right under any creed of the protestant faith.